Stop Managing Volunteers!

New Competencies
for
Volunteer
Administrators

by

Sue Vineyard

Graphic Design by Scott Hoffman

00000
A Teaching Text & Workbook

Heritage Arts Publishing
1807 Prairie Avenue
Downers Grove, Illinois 60515
964-1194*

*Area code 708 until 8/96; after that: 630.

ISBN # 0-911029-44-3
c. Sue Vineyard 1996

Sue Vineyard is the author of:

Finding Your Way Through the Maze of Volunteer Management*
Fundraising for Hospices*
Beyond Banquets, Plaques & Pins: Creative Ways to Recognize Volunteers
Marketing Magic for Volunteer Programs
101 Ideas for Volunteer Programs**
Evaluating Volunteers, Programs & Events
101 Ways to Raise Resources**
Secrets of Motivation: How to Get and Keep Volunteers and Paid Staff
How to Take Care of You, So You Can Take Care of Others
101 Tips for Volunteer Recruitment**
Secrets of Leadership
Managing Volunteer Diversity: A Rainbow of Opportunities**
Resource Directory for Volunteer Programs*
Basic Volunteer Management Training Kit
The Great Trainer's Guide: How to Train (almost) Anyone to do (almost) Anything!
Megatrends & Volunteerism: Mapping the Future of Volunteer Programs
101 MORE Ideas for Volunteer Programs**

Plus two audios: "Care for the Caregiver" & "Surviving Burnout"
and one video: "Building a Bridge from Dream to Reality: The Basics of Volunteer Management"

She is also the founding and Senior Editor of the major newsletter in the field:
"GRAPEVINE: Volunteerism's Newsletter"**

ii.

*out of print   **with Steve McCurley

How to Use This Book.....

In an attempt to reduce any questions or frustrations you might have as you use this book, let me give you some insight into my thinking as I chose format, phrases and wordings:

Gender: I decided to refer to those who lead volunteer programs as "she" rather than the clumsy "he/she" phrase because 90% of the people who hold these positions are women. I am pleased to see men in the field, we need more of them, but until the majority are male, I'll stick with female references knowing that the men will be as forgiving of the slight as women have been through all of literature's history. Thank you.

Title: Selecting one consistent title for people who lead volunteer programs kept me up at night! I therefore swing back and forth between volunteer administrator, volunteer program leader and volunteer director. Sometimes I even used the title found mostly in hospital settings: DVS, standing for "Directors of Volunteer Services." You need to insert whatever title you have or feel comfortable with. This makes the book a collaboration between us, so welcome and thank you! (I still prefer the title I introduced two books ago: "Volunteer Program Executive" but wiser heads said "the field's not there yet, Sue." so I defer to their wisdom.)

Who? When I don't specify whether a point is aimed at volunteers or paid staff, I'm signaling you that it can apply to either.

References: You'll find them at the back of the book in the Bibliography.

Worksheets: The Teaching Text shows references in parenthesis that refer to a worksheet which takes the concept taught in the text to the next level by offering readers a tool to apply the learning to their own program. Worksheets immediately follow the Teaching Text in each chapter. I suggest you photocopy these worksheets for continuing use.

This book comes after many requests from people in the field to give them a tool that offers learning and then helps the reader transfer the learning to their own situation. I've written it with the hope that it will do just that and that, as mature adult readers, you will lay aside those ideas that would not work for you and feast instead on those that might. Let me know how you like this format; I have several other topics running around in my head that might lend themselves to this format if it is helpful to readers.

Be well......

Sue Vineyard
March 1996

iii.

great thanks

to Betty Greer and Mary Wiser who spent their invaluable time combing my manuscript and offering suggestions. They keep me honest, hold my feet to the fire and teach me much about the changing challenges of volunteer administration. Even more importantly, they are my friends.

Thank you.

INDEX

Worksheets follow at the end of each Chapter and are coded with the Chapter number and the sequential number of that worksheet, thus the 1st worksheet in Chapter One is coded:(1-1); the 6th worksheet in Chapter Ten is coded:(10-6) etc.

Chapter One

STOP MANAGING VOLUNTEERS!

> *** Reminder: You'll immedediately see references to the worksheets that are found at the end of each chapter. Each is identified with the chapter number & worksheet sequence, thus the 1st worksheet for this chapter is (1-1); the 5th, (1-5) etc., These worksheets help you to apply specific learnings to your own circumstances.**

That's right, stop managing volunteers. After more than two dozen years of teaching folks how to manage volunteers, I really am telling you to STOP! But before you impeach me on grounds of heresy or condemn me for betrayal, take a look at the meaning of this admonition..........

In today's faster-than-a-speeding-bullet world, where volunteers have new adjectives to describe their service such as 'episodic', 'hit & run', 'entrepreneurial' or 'service-learning', our methods of directing volunteers have to be reshaped, with updated responses, behaviors and patterns. We must develop new competencies to meet new demands.

To borrow a popular phrase from the business sector of today, we have to "Re-invent our organizations!"

Where once the symbols of a heart and a hand could depict volunteerism, now a more appropriate graphic might be a kaleidoscope with it's ever-changing shapes, colors and configurations.

Polly Do-Gooder.... that white, upper-class, suburban housewife dying to be elected president of the Garden Club or chair of the church Lady's Aide committee.... is dead or at the very least off closing a take-over deal between two business conglomerates. The volunteer of today is more likely to be found organizing other residents in her housing project as they work to take over the complex and rid it of drug dealers and guns.

Or maybe Polly has 'morphed' into Paulo who has formed a safety-watch organization in the inner city that has seen a 40% drop in street crime since it came on the scene...... or she's just 14 and part of a school-based service-learning project that helps Habitat for Humanity rehab houses or possibly she's 19 and a part of the Delta Service Corps working to bring literacy to adults in a small Mississippi River town as she earns credit that will allow her to attend college a year from now.

Woodie Guthrie was right: "The times they are a'changing."

As leaders of volunteer programs, organizations and agencies, we too must also change. We must inventory (1-1) what actions we have used in the past, sorting through our list to preserve those parts (1-2) that remain relevant and designing new ones to replace the ones that no longer work. We must look to every other sector of our society to see what strategies are being used that might be transferable to our work and help us be more effective. (1-3)

We have to be brave enough to examine every assumption on which our current work, methods and policies are based and ask ourselves, "Is that assumption still accurate today?" We must leave no stone unturned, no corner unexplored, no sacred cows avoided in our quest for relevancy.

We have to do our homework, identifying the information (1-4) we need to keep up to date with the changes in the general population and our own specific client and worker base to insure that *what* we are offering and *how* we are offering it matches the needs, wants and characteristics of these constituents.

Nothing is sadder than a conversation I occasionally have with Volunteer Directors who call to complain that they are simply not getting the respect they deserve; that their volunteer program was once the shining star of their larger organization but has fallen into an after-thought by the administration. Usually, they have a long list of reasons this has happened..... shrinking resources, demands by top brass for "bottom-line" thinking, volunteer-staff discord, their long-time, stalwart volunteers retiring, moving away, or dying and the oft-heard wail that volunteers don't want to really commit themselves as they used to.

Fortunately these conversations do not happen very frequently any more, as the program leaders of today recognize the shifting patterns (1-5) of volunteerism and have adjusted accordingly. When speaking with these highly successful, newly-changed volunteer program administrators, I hear a major shift in how they are spending their time:

They don't directly manage volunteers!

They do:

1: **Concentrate on establishing systems** that support the volunteer's work in the organization. For example: Directors of Volunteer Services (DVS) in hospitals work with the department heads around the facility who will have volunteers in their arena. They also work directly with the staff persons who will supervise the various volunteers to insure that procedures and expectations are realistic and that placement is an appropriate "fit". (1-6;1-7;1-8)

2: **Constantly assess needs** in the organization to see where volunteers might be helpful, where they would not be appropriate and what special skills are required for a successful placement. (1-9)

3: **Keep up to date** on demographics and trends in the general population so that any necessary shifts can be made in recruiting, training and direction volunteers.

Every few years leaders challenge key people to look honestly at every assumption, conclusion and habit on which current work is based in order that they might root out those which no longer fit the times or organization. They are willing to risk major change to sweep out inappropriate behaviors and establish new patterns that match the needs of today.

4. **Work to insure** that the organizational hierarchy, leadership and other executive levels of their agency **recognize the contributions** that volunteers make both at their work and within the larger community as they become ambassadors for the organization. They stay highly visible, never allowing leaders to take volunteers for granted, underestimate their value or the value of the DVS herself in orchestrating their whole-organization integration. (1-10) They also find innovative ways to help volunteers do the same as <u>they</u> interact with decision-makers in the community and within the organization itself.

5. **Keep bottom-line figures in their head.** Even if they are not number-people themselves, they have someone around them who is and can teach them the facts and figures. At any challenge, therefore, by bean-counters or frightened CEOs whose Board has told them to "cut back", they can show real results of the value of volunteer's time investment, the national figures showing that volunteers donate twice as much as non-volunteers and the correlation between giving and volunteering. (1-11) Wise DVS's keep a file at the ready to document how invaluable volunteers are and what the institution might look like without volunteers, showing contributions by much more than just hours.

6. **Insure** that constant, varied and **appropriate recognition** is interwoven throughout the entire year to highlight both volunteers and staff work, drop-in and on-going volunteers, innovative ideas and services created, and other unique contributions. The banquet at the end of the year is never canceled, but it becomes only one of hundreds of ways DVSs find to say thank you to volunteers, staff, supporters, board members and administrators.

7. **Pay attention to the public's perception** of their program, making friends with media and PR folks who can tell their story in human terms, knowing that such publicity can generate interest and possible connections for future volunteers, clients, paid staff, suppliers and supporters. (1-12) They often work with the agency's marketing staff to assist in getting program stories to the public in order to help shape the perception

8. **Work to keep things simple**. Life is complex enough without systems, procedures and secret compartments of information that look like a maze. They constantly strive to simplify work, keeping their eye on the mission of volunteering in their agency.

9. **Work to break down barriers**, eliminate fences, disrupt cliques, open communication and reject negativity that comes from tyranny by a handful of prima donna's who insist everything must be done their way. They believe in democracy and the possibilities in change and demonstrate this belief.(1-13)

10. **Always, always, always keep their eye on the vision** of the agency as a whole and the role volunteers can play to achieve that vision. They can articulate simply and quickly what that vision is and get others to catch sight of it. They measure all decisions and actions against it and are constantly stretching to improve performance that will lead to the vision. They are fanatical about keeping the vision foremost in everyone's mind and find new ways to insure everything is "mission-driven".(1-14)

11. **Attend to the climate**, or "feel" of the part of the organization under their direction in order to keep it as healthy as possible. Wellness of both the program and its people is upper-most in the mind of the DVS who constantly monitors it to keep it healthy. Ethical decision making, fairness and principled values (1-15) are used as thermometers to test for wellness and anyone exhibiting signs of back-biting, score-keeping, rumor-mongering or prejudice are quickly banished..... no ifs, ands or buts, and absolutely no dancing with the devil and being "Mrs. Nice-Nice" at all costs! Misinformation is corrected immediately and dis-information leads to instant reprimand and possible dismissal for the person spreading it.

12. **Work to establish solid, healthy relationships** and partnerships (1-16) among all who interact with the program..... volunteers, paid staff, board members, suppliers, supporters, etc. The volunteer administrator recognizes that relationships are a primary demand of adults today and therefore focuses on ways to create, support and strengthen connectedness between people and efforts.

In all of this, you will note one glaring omission. She does not spend her time trying to manage the day to day work of volunteers. Her relationship to volunteers is more triangular than linear. She brings volunteers into the agency, identifying the best possible placement and then works with the staff members and/or volunteer leaders who will directly supervise them in order that the relationship between the volunteers and their supervisors is the best it can be. (1-17)

As programs grow and staff supervise multiple volunteers, the volunteer program executive may even withdraw one layer more, working with the supervisor of several staff who work directly with volunteers. When programs reach numbers such as 500 or 600 volunteers working directly with 50-60 staff members who in turn, are supervised by 5 or 6 directors, it makes sense to work through the smaller number to affect the vast cadre serving clients.

BUT A WORD OF CAUTION....the further away you are from the volunteer's actual work, the more you must do to insure that you are still very much in touch with the demands on workers, working conditions and especially, any changing risks that might be encountered. Stay in touch with what's happening on the job! Without that realistic understanding of what is needed, you cannot recruit, place, train, recognize or oversee volunteers efforts successfully.

Also accept the fact that no matter how much is delegated within the organization, the DVS is still accountable for what volunteers do.

And one last tidbit before we move on to greater specifics of competencies and strategies you as a volunteer program administrator will have to use if you are to lead the effective deployment of volunteer energies throughout your agency (1-18):

You'll have to know how to manage volunteers!

Huh? But this chapter is entitled "STOP Managing Volunteers!" ....

As the late comedian Gilda Radner often said, ... "Oh, never mind........"

Even though the successful volunteer program administrator should not be spending the majority of her time directly supervising all volunteers, she still needs to know HOW to manage their efforts.

She will need to demonstrate this expertise by directly planning, organizing, staffing, supervising and evaluating the small number of volunteers who might work in her office. This demonstration can then serve as a model as she trains paid staff to work with the volunteers assigned to them.

Understanding the basics of managing volunteers (or paid staff: the process is the same) is still critical to the success of program administrators as they coach those needing such skills.

So, by this time, my message should be quite clear:

Stop managing volunteers.

Learn how to manage volunteers.

You're right, Gilda.....just never mind........

Skills Inventory

The following skills are commonly thought to be the "basics" needed to effectively lead a volunteer program. Check those which you believe have brought your program to this point; then check those which you believe you will need to rely on most heavily to lead your program into the future. Finally, rank your level of expertise for each skill.

Skill	Used to Present	Need for Future	Personal Expertise:			
			High	Average	Low	Need to Strengthen
Diplomacy						
Servant hood						
Advocacy						
Personnel Management						
Visioning						
Assertiveness						
Manage Details						
Conflict Resolution						
Delegation						
Fund Raising						
Event Planning						
Recruitment						
Recognition						
Problem Solving						
Problem Analysis						
Juggle Demands						
Time Management						
Prioritization						
Crisis Management						
Risk Management						
Planning						
Organizing						
Placement						
Training						
Evaluating						
Coaching						
Finance & Budgeting						
Administration						
Supervising						
Add Your Own:						

Skills Development

Look at the Skills Inventory (1-1). What <u>additional</u> skills are you going to need to help your program grow stronger?

Skills Needed:

How will you develop each skill? Set a timeline for development of each:

Of those skills you listed in worksheet 1-1 that need to be developed or strengthened, how do you plan to do so for each? By when? How are you going to measure your progress?

Transferable Skills

Look around at other professions, efforts and societal movement. What strategies and skills do you find there that you might adapt to your work? Example: "Bench marking" has become widely used in automotive manufacturing as a way to keep standards of workmanship high. How might you identify bench marks in the arena of volunteer program management and work toward these standards?

Watch for examples of transferable learnings continually. Typically they will address such issues as motivation, quality, creativity, problem-solving, improvement, communication, team-building, interaction, rewards, public relations, etc.

Keep your eyes open for great ideas that you can adapt!!

Doing Our Homework

Good leadership begins with good information which is constantly updated. As you plan activities, do your homework to get the facts and demographics on:

General Population: (Stats are available through Chamber of Commerce, Mayor's offices, etc.)

Total population in your service area: Median age:

Median income: Income range:

Growth potential:

	Now	1 year	5 years	10 years	20 years
General population:					
Client population:					
Volunteer involved:					
Paid staff:					

Trends: What major trends are present in your area that impact your program's clients, services, volunteers, paid staff, etc? (i.e.: An area dependent on one major factory which is closing its doors.)

What general trends impact your program? (i.e.: Working women, youthful population, etc.)

As you note information, consider your response options (i.e.: working women need shorter work assignments as volunteers, flex-time and space, etc.)

Shifting Volunteer Patterns

Most volunteer program administrators recognize shifts in patterns of volunteering. What have you seen? How have you or your predecessors adapted to these shifts? What new responses can you design? What further shifts do you anticipate?

Historically, change occurs at a more rapid rate as you approach the end of one century and the beginning of another. Be alert for shifting patterns. Anticipate change and be ready with creative responses!

Responsibility Audit (Part I)

A growing trend in salary and benefit negotiation is the relating of compensation to the responsibilities individual workers and/or departments have within an organization. Identifying the responsibilities you, your key people (volunteer & paid) and department have is a good exercise no matter what the motivation, because it clarifies all that falls under your jurisdiction.

Such information can be helpful when negotiating with others for support, recruiting volunteers or paid staff, public relations, planning, recognition, accountability, friend-raising or you own career development, among other things.

As responsibilities change, you will need to update your information. Each time you do so, you may amaze even yourself in seeing all that falls under your leadership. Use the following as a guideline for examination:

	Self	Key People	Department
Major Responsibilities:			

Primary Goals:

Key People Supervised, & Responsibilities:

Budget:
    Income:

    Expenses:

Clients Served:

Timelines:

Other Demands:

Responsibility Audit (Part II)

As important as it is to be clear on what your responsibilities ARE, it is also important to identify what things are NOT under your control but still impact your work:

....

| Things controlled by other people: | Who controls this? | What influence do you have with these people? | How can you impact this? |

....

....

Systems

Overseeing the systems that support volunteer involvement throughout your organization is a critical part of the modern effective volunteer program administrator's responsibility. What systems are in place that support volunteering? What others are needed?

List systems now in place that effect volunteers:

Check those which are empowering and help volunteers be effective. How can you protect and enhance these positive systems?

Which are either impractical, out-of-date, or for some reason, get in the way of smooth integration of volunteers and staff trying to accomplish objectives? How can you make them better or get rid of them? Who might object to your changing these systems? How can you remove their objections?

Internal Needs Assessment

List current placements of volunteers (by area, department or specific job), and then identify where volunteers could be of value but are not now involved. DO NOT make negative assumptions for others (i.e.: "They'd never accept volunteers.") Think instead of where appropriate volunteers could work in furthering the mission of the organization...you can strategize how to make this happen later!

Where are volunteers working now? What do they do? How many? Who supervises them?

Are there places in the organization where volunteers do not now work? Could they be appropriate for capable volunteers? Who controls these areas and what needs might they have that could be met by volunteers?

....

Area:	Supervisor:	Needs:	Skills required:	Best approach to Superv.

....

....

Recognizing Contributions

Document the contributions of your volunteers to the overall mission of your organization. Then find ways to bring these to the attention of your administration, supporters and general public. It's critical for your department's contributions to be seen!

Ways volunteers support the work and mission of your organization: (Think in terms of energy, specific work, contributions, etc. Do not think only in terms of hours donated or its dollar value.)

Ways volunteers are ambassadors for your organization in the greater community:

How you encourage volunteers to act as ambassadors for your organization:

Bottom-line Figures

It is critical to keep some figures at your fingertips. No matter how painful for those who dreaded math or accounting courses, certain numbers must be learned and recalled. Create a list that is specific to your program, to include:

Number of volunteers per year:

Number of hours served collectively:

Value of volunteer time:*

Replacement costs to pay workers for same efforts:

Budget for your department:

Increase/decrease year to year for your budget over last five years:

Budget increase/decrease vs. increase/decreased of number of volunteers and number of clients:

Overall budget for entire organization: % to volunteer department:

Any income generated by volunteers through products, sales etc:

Income generated by volunteers through donations or capitol campaigns:

Overhead costs of generating income in previous two questions:

Volunteers have proven* to give three times more in donations than "non-volunteers"; can you point to any direct gifts given ($, goods, etc.) by volunteers who are involved with you?

* Independent Sector of Washington, DC offers statistics in their bi-annual Gallup Poll, Giving and Volunteering. Keep up-to-date on these changing figures. Hourly wage figures come from the annual President's Economic Report showing the rate for non-agricultural workers.

Perceptions

Public Perceptions:

How the public "sees" your efforts determines to great extent how they support and interact with you. Keep your eye on public perceptions:

How do you tell your story to the public regarding what your volunteers are doing?

What media do you use? Who are key media people who you work with?

What additional ways can you devise to tell others what you do to serve the community?

How do you measure public perception of your work? What is it?

How can you strengthen good and accurate public perceptions? Reduce poor ones?

Internal Perception: In larger organizations, you will need to measure how others see your work:

What is the internal perception of your department? How do you know this?

What is the general attitude about volunteers? It this fair & accurate?

If there are misconceptions, how can you change these?

What key people might help you sharpen the internal perceptions regarding volunteers & your department? How can you influence them? How can volunteer energies help them directly?

Barriers

What "barriers" now exist that make it difficult to:

1. Become a volunteer for your program:

2. Get appropriate work assignments:

3. Work as a volunteer:

4. Work with paid staff:

5. Receive appropriate recognition:

6. Become equipped to do a good job:

7. Find satisfaction as a volunteer:

8. Fit into assignments:

9. Leave:

10. Find acceptance with existing volunteers:

11. Suggest changes:

12: Get good information to yourself or others:

13: Others, specific to your program:

Vision

What is the overall mission or vision of your organization?

What is the mission of your department?

How **can** the above be expressed simply and clearly to others?

How **is** the mission expressed now?

What new ways can you devise to insure the vision is clearly expressed to others? How can people be reminded of it continually?

Values

What values do your organization and/or department hold dear? (i.e.: open communication.)

Which values impact the way decisions are made? (i.e.: a high value on open communication typically leads to decisions being made with effected parties input.)

Which values dictate ethics in your organization? (i.e.: open communication leads to an ethical philosophy of honest.)

What actions are forbidden because they oppose identified values? (i.e.: a high value of honesty means dishonesty is not tolerated.)

Relationships

Who are key "others" with whom you must relate and interact within your organization and department? What is your present relationship with each? How can you enhance each relationship genuinely?

Key People:	Responsibility:	Current Relationship:	How Enhance?

What might each need that you could provide? (i.e.: support doing paperwork, filling quota of work, solve problems, etc.)

*Keep in mind that good relationships must be genuine; both parties must sense honest caring.

Time Audit

How much time do you now spend in direct supervision of volunteers? Track the time you spend:

Supervising:

Training:

Coaching:

Orienting:

Planning with:

Doing specific work assignments with:

Interviewing:

Placing:

Planning:

Evaluating:

Recognizing:

Totally, what % of your time is given to <u>directly</u> working with volunteers?

What % of your time is given to working with staff to facilitate <u>their</u> direct management of volunteers?

Staying Connected

As your time is diverted from working directly with volunteers and spent instead working with paid staff who supervise volunteers, you will need to keep "up" with what is required of these volunteers.

How can you stay in touch with the demands on volunteers and what they are being asked to do, what they experience and what they are exposed to?

Chapter Two

Working with Staff

There is no greater example of how our field of managing volunteers has changed than is found in our relationship to paid staff. Where before our competencies needed to be in managing volunteers, it now must shift over to working with paid staff who work directly with volunteers.

Where once our work with the majority of our volunteers was linear and direct, it now is better diagrammed by a triangular relationship, with volunteer administrators working most directly with staff who in turn work directly with volunteers.

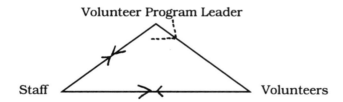

This reality dramatically changes the demands on the volunteer program leader and re-defines the roles she must play and the competencies she must have. Let's compare the older definition of a volunteer director and the newer one in the light of this paradigm shift:

Primary competencies needed in the past:

    Management of volunteers: Planning, Organizing, Staffing, Supervising, Assessing
    Motivation
    Recognition
    Communication
    Leadership
    Accountability

Now, IN ADDITION to (not instead of) the above, she must also add:

Coaching
Consulting
Risk Management
Public Relations
Resource development
Leveraging for decision-making (empowerment) positions
Climate control
Visioning

Many of you had already worked your way into the arena of these skills, some without even labeling them as I have and mixed them with the competencies you had developed long ago. I was privileged to run into such program leaders as Mary Wiser at Courage Center near Minneapolis/St. Paul and Betty Greer at Rex and Mission hospitals in North Carolina, but they were the exception, not the rule.

Outstanding volunteer program leaders seemed to have learned innately to position themselves as internal consultants within their organizations; dealing directly with the staff members who would direct volunteer activities. They were directly involved with the intake and placement decisions of volunteers to enable the best possible match-up between volunteer skills and staff needs.

Universally, such outstanding professionals turned their attention to:

☞ Appropriate recruitment, making sure messages were precise, accurate & targeted.

☞ Overseeing the interviewing to insure good information about recruits and proper screening.

☞ Going directly to department heads and people in authority to find out what their needs were, listening for clues for how volunteers might be helpful.

☞ Weighing risk management factors before any placement of volunteers.

☞ Overseeing appropriate orientation of volunteers as well as coaching paid staff on how to train them for specific work assignments.

☞ Monitoring exit interviews to constantly upgrade volunteer placement.

☞ Finding ways to become part of the decision-making mechanism in the wider agency so that they could be proactive in issues that impact volunteers and suggest ways that volunteers might be integrated in the new locations to meet needs expressed by staff.

☞ Orchestrating recognition, not just of volunteers, but of paid staff who demonstrated outstanding skills in working with volunteers.

☞ Constantly campaigning (subtly and overtly) to have staff and administration see volunteers as an integrated part of every corner of the agency rather than a "department" that is separate and therefore in competition with other departments. They work toward having their department seen as a team player for others.

☞ Continually keeping their eye on the pulse of community needs, understanding that volunteers can be representatives of the organization when they are out in the community and can report back on new needs they are seeing. As this has become more and more of a measuring stick (finding new needs in a community, reporting back to an organization and then helping to devise responses to such needs) for non-profit status, it has taken on new importance.

☞ Keeping eyes and ears open for changes in the wider arenas of litigation, risk management, governing mandates, etc. and adjusting work accordingly; a watch-dog role to protect the work and workers of the organization.

☞ Documenting efforts of screening, training, supervising and managing volunteers as protection against any possible accusations of mis-conduct; careful assessment of any volunteer roles that were once paid positions to avoid conflict with unions, etc.

☞ Insuring that everyone hears about the great job volunteers are doing; they recognize it is dangerous for anyone to underestimate the value of volunteers or have them ever seen as an "expendable expense."

The list can go on. You probably would add a few I've missed, and I urge you to do so, as you sketch out how much the role of the volunteer program administrator has changed over the last 30 years. Each characteristic you add points to another competency needed in the search for excellence.

None may be more important than their work as an internal consultant who works with staff on behalf of volunteers, and understanding what that role of consultant means. Let's look at some characteristics of good consultants who.........

#1. *Are clear communicators.* They listen intently and speak clearly, typically using word economy. They never use quarter words when nickel ones will do. They listen intently to understand needs rather than trying to impress others with how much they know. When gathering information, they use feedback to insure that they understood what was intended.

#2. *Go slowly.* They do not jump to conclusions and never "take sides" in a dispute. They get input from every perspective available before drawing conclusions. When they cannot get to the bottom of a need or problem, they keep digging until it becomes clear.

#3. *Offer options for action* and are willing and even eager to fine tune their suggestions if implementors see flaws in their thinking. They are secure and flexible enough to adjust what they first proposed. They do not take rejection of their suggestions personally but rather as a challenge or opportunity to learn.

#4. *Can let go* of the ideas and see others implement them. They do not have to be thanked when the effort is successful; just knowing they were a part of the beginning focus is satisfying enough. They see ideas as public currency, not "theirs" alone.

#5. *Can adjust* their style of coaching to the learning style of the people being coached. If one person learns best through demonstration, they demonstrate; if another learns best by reading instructions, they write them down; if a third learns best through discussion, they discuss.

#6. *Are always listening* for changing information so that they can suggest new ways to integrate volunteers throughout the organization They appreciate the power in careful timing and understand that what may be obvious to them about how volunteers can serve may NOT be obvious to others. They find innovative ways to help others devise volunteer involvements and feel ownership of such involvement.

#7. *Know how to invest* those staff members who will be working with volunteers directly; they are good strategizers and would typically get "A's" in reading people!

#8. *Adopt an attitude of servant-leader* and work hard to be seen as professional, caring and well-informed. They are sincere and truly believe in the power of volunteerism.

#9. *Transfer learning constantly....* from other fields to their own work; from their heads and knowledge base to that of others; from data others may overlook; from any one source to another they believe would benefit from such transfer They are a constant access to the information highway!

#10. *Know when to be formal in their consultant relationships and when to be informal;* their actions are appropriate to the topic, people involved and issues at hand.

#11. *Constantly upgrade their own skills* and work to bring new learnings to their assignments. They avoid ruts and only examine new management and leadership fads of the day for any application to the consultant role they have with staff in their own agency; they are not impressed with gimmicks. They can take the long view; quick Band-Aids are not their style although they can suggest quick-fixes for immediate emergencies.

#12. *Stay physically, emotionally, spiritually and mentally healthy;* they understand that taking care of themselves is not a luxury but a necessary requirement if they are to be as effective as possible.

#13. *Never play favorites,* even when they have them. They are fair and open to everyone; they see their neutrality as an insurance that people from all perspectives will trust them. They understand that their reputation as a fair, equitable, calm problem-solver is only as good at their last interaction, so they are careful in what they do or say. They never break confidences and always protect information sources on sensitive issues.

#14. *Never bow to tyranny of the minority;* They easily spot those who want to bully or unfairly influence their conclusions and are careful to stay focused on objective suggestions. They are realistic and try to help others deal effectively with the challenges of having to work around tyrants.

#15. *Know when they are in over their heads;* they call in experts when they cannot solve a problem. They do not feel they must have "all the answers" and do not see asking for help as a weakness.

#16. *Take the responsibility that is rightly theirs* when things go wrong after others took their advice. They never blame others, but look for positive new approaches to overcome any difficulties. They are problem-assessors and solvers; they have the ability to scrape off symptoms to find root causes. They see blaming and poor-me wallowing as a waste of time; they hate whining.

#17. *Can juggle many demands* from many different areas at once; they do not confuse their priorities and can quickly see what comes first, second, etc. in their work.

Again, the list can go on. As you slip into the role of internal consultant in your organization, working directly with staff who work with volunteers, you will identify other characteristics you must have if you are to be successful in your particular placement.

Some of the attached worksheets will help you identify attitudes and strategies you can use in this widening role as you rise to new levels of competency in this area.(2-1; 2-2, etc.)

None may be more important for your future.

Staff Assessment Survey on Volunteer Involvement

Complete the Following questionnaire. This survey will assess readiness to utilize volunteers and determine what is needed to ensure continued delivery of high quality service to our clientele. All of the information collected will be kept confidential.

I. Your Previous Experience with Volunteers

1. Have you previously worked in an agency which utilized volunteers?

   ❑ Yes   ❑ No   ❑ Don't know

2. Have you previously supervised any volunteers?

   ❑ Yes   ❑ No   ❑ Don't know

3. Do you do any volunteer work yourself?

   ❑ Yes   ❑ No   ❑ Once did, but not any more

II. Your Assessment of Volunteer Involvement

1. What is your overall assessment of the desirability of utilizing volunteers in our agency now?

   ❑ Very desirable   ❑ Somewhat desirable   ❑ Uncertain
   ❑ Not desirable at this time   ❑ Would never be appropriate

2. What is your overall assessment of our current readiness to utilize volunteers?

   ❑ Very ready   ❑ Somewhat ready   ❑ Uncertain   ❑ Not ready

3. Are there any types of work for which you think volunteers are particularly needed & suited?

4. Are there any areas or types of work you believe volunteers should NOT do in our agency?

5. What issues or concerns would you like to see addressed before we involve volunteers?

6. What type of training or assistance would you like to receive before you are asked to work with volunteers?

7. Are there any other comments or suggestions you would like to express about the involvement of volunteers in our agency?

Used with permission: Volunteer Management, 1996. c. Steve McCurley & Rick Lynch

Resistant Staff Role Play

To be used with staff who might harbor resistance to volunteers being involved in agency efforts:

Unspoken Concerns and Agendas:

#1:   'Everyone seems to want to eat lunch with the new volunteer; they ignore me. She's probably more interesting than I am because she's had so many wonderful experiences in her life while I've been stuck in this boring job, just trying to make ends meet.'

❧ Things you want to point out to those you are training with this role play include:
1. Expression of loneliness/abandonment..."they ignore me."
2. Assumption that the volunteer has had a wonderful life & lots of great experiences.
3. Feeling that their own work is boring.
4. "Poor me", victim posture..."just trying to make ends meet; boring job."

#2:   'I'm so worried about my teenager at home who's nearly failing out of school and is hanging out with a bunch of druggies. My concentration is falling apart and now they want me to focus and teach a volunteer how to do this job. The pressure is building and I can't even keep my mind on my work as it is now!'

❧ Things you want to point out:
1. May feel they are not thought of as a whole person, with some life outside work.
2. Assumption that volunteer will be more trouble than is worth it.
3. Hidden fear that they will teach the volunteer "how to do (MY) job" and maybe lose it?
4. Possible assumption that volunteers come with no skills.

#3:   ' So they've found a retired expert to help me. Swell. I suppose he knows all the answers and I'll look stupid next to him. Right now I'm pretty respected in the office, but now this guy will show me up. Maybe they'll want him permanently, then I'll be out pounding the pavement looking for a new job.'

❧ Things you may want to point out:
1. Person has done "negative head-talk" thinking; assumes the worst.
2. Projects to a position of victim, thus creating an adversarial role between volunteer & self.
3. Fears loss of prestige and looking "stupid"; loss of respect.
4. Fears losing job to volunteer; assumes volunteer has greater expertise.

#4:   'Lucky me. I get a volunteer. Big deal. Are they going to give the volunteer the best part of my job? Hey, if they take part of my job away from me, are they going to figure I'm not worth so much and lower my pay? I sure wish someone around here would have asked me if I even wanted a volunteer!! Maybe they're trying to edge me out.'

❧ Things you may want to point out:
1. This person also fears loss of job; national statistics show less than 1% of volunteers take a paid worker's place. It's violates contract & is diligently watched by unions, etc.
2. They are projecting negatively that volunteers are there to "take part of my job."
4. Expressions of fear of less compensation, which may be equated to less personal worth.
3. They are expressing frustration at not being part of the decision to involve volunteers

Chapter Three

ENTER:
"LEADERSHIFT"

There seems to be a fetish of late that causes people to come up with a new management-gimmick-of-the-month that is packaged and sold as every organization's cure-all for blemishes, warts and in-grown dysfunction. Those who devise them can make a bundle selling books, giving lectures, consulting and producing video and audio tapes that offer their organizational-elixirs in easy-to-swallow form. (3-1)

I have good news and bad news about these "cure-alls":

Some of them work. Some don't. Off and on.

If you examine the basis of almost all of the newer strategies in management that corporations adopt as their savior-of-the-month, you begin to notice something familiar:

> They are all rooted in treating people kindly, fairly and with an assumption that workers are dedicated, intelligent beings with something to offer, especially when equipped with good information and the tools & permissions to make things happen and that the customer is the reason for doing anything.

Sounds a lot like the base on which leadership of volunteers has been built for centuries:

**People empowered to be successful and respected/thanked
for their contributions as they work for the good of their clients.**

Successful volunteer programs are typically rooted in keeping that simple definition as a golden rule. They are also typically led by someone who examines all the latest management fads and identifies those parts that are transferable and valuable to the jobs at hand. This leader is wise enough to be able to shift from one tool to another as needed, just as she shifts people from one place to another to create the most effective project teams.

I call this flexibility "Leadershift" and see it as one of the competencies volunteer program leaders must have to successfully achieve goals.

If you need a definition, try this one on for size:

"Leadershift is the ability to adapt by moving people and things around in order to accomplish changing goals."

The only problem in giving you this definition is **it** can change, as for example, you need to shift ideas, information, and even objects around to accomplish emerging needs. It may mean shifting your own leadership style or management posture as different people and circumstances change. One day you may need to dictate actions (ie: risk management rules) the next day you need to play the role of Expert and a third day you may need to withdraw to the role of Absentee Ruler; one day leader, the next day follower. (3-2)

The whole idea of Leadershift is that you can legitimately shift anything and anyone around to suit needs. The guiding principle behind this is simply a healthy dose of common sense which can tell you when changing is good and when it is not. It also means erasing old tapes, keeping an open mind and being brave enough to move out of comfortable ruts.

Leadershift also demands that you have a clear vision of several of its inherent characteristics, because it is more of an attitude than a process, and is therefore dependent on people's spirit in using it. Let's look at each:

Characteristic #1: **"Please Pass the Baton"**

The first characteristic that comes from adopting an attitude of Leadershift is the empowering of people to lead from their own strength in a setting with others who have been brought together to tackle a problem or need.

Through Leadershift, you as the program leader, would gather those individuals from any arena...(read on for a definition of "boundaryless behavior" and you will see that I really mean ANY arena.) who could bring a needed perspective to the task at hand.

Let me use an example:

My husband and I recently bought a home in Door County, Wisconsin. We're right on the shores of the Green Bay waters near a wonderfully quaint town, population: 182, called Egg Harbor. Door County is the midwest's most popular tourist site with it's centuries-old fishing villages reminiscent of Cape Cod.

Several leaders in our area have decided to form a volunteer center there to coordinate services, volunteer opportunities and to create a group of volunteer directors who can support one another personally and professionally. (What Dr. Ivan Scheier, a pioneer in volunteer leadership would call a DOVIA...Directors of Volunteers in Agencies.)

If Leadershift was being used to establish this entity, someone takes the role of the ultimate leader. There is always an ultimate leader in making things happen. Traditionally it is the person who has final responsibility to see that things begin and continue appropriately toward the vision. Often it is the person who first presents the vision to others. (3-3)

The "players" in this effort would possibly look like this:

Ultimate Leader: The person who first has the vision and can cause others to catch sight of this vision in such a way that they wish to become involved. She enables the first meeting and asks others to help decide who needs to attend.

Co-founders: Those whom the ultimate leader first finds most interested in the project. They each have a stake in the success of this venture and will benefit directly. They bring skills, contacts and a willingness to make it happen.

Community Leaders: Those carefully recruited who have the interest of the general population at heart and can see the wisdom and need for the volunteer center. They have many contacts in the area which can be helpful as the center gets underway.

Specialists: Those people identified by the ultimate leader and co-founders who have the specific skills the leadership believes it will need to get a volunteer center going.....an accountant, a banker, an attorney and possibly an expert in group dynamics, planning and volunteerism if they are available.

Representatives: In anticipation of a variety of types of volunteerism being served, representatives from those categories are invited to the meeting to lend their perspective: Hospital and health care, abuse centers, community organizations, the schools, arts, literacy, emergency relief, national groups, charities, fund raising groups, corporate programs, military (the Coast Guard is stationed in Door County), welfare agencies, municipal and state agencies, self help groups, historical societies, wildlife groups, sports & fitness programs, etc. etc.

Led by the ultimate leader, the first meeting would be held and open to the public to see who else might be attracted and why. The leader would explain the concept and vision of a volunteer center, then ask for input from those present as to how this might benefit their work and what they could lend to the effort.

Suggestions would come from co-founders as to procedures for continuing, with a founder's committee and an advisory committee being established. Next meetings would be set and goals established for what each person was to do prior to those meetings. Suggestions for enlisting others would be asked for and follow-up to inviting them would be planned.

When the second meetings were about to be held, the ultimate leaders (remember, you now have two committees...planning and advisory) would send an agenda telling everyone's role, who would attend and when/where it would be held.

At those meetings the ultimate leader would call on each person and TURN THE LEADERSHIP OVER TO THEM WHILE THEY REPORTED ON THEIR RESULTS.

This is the essential quality of Leader*shift*....that the leader role shifts to the person speaking about their efforts in the whole project. As work continues, different perspectives would be called for, and others invited to join the effort who could speak to their perspective. This might include clients, business owners, CEOs of agencies, etc.

When these different people share their perspective of the work, THEY become the leader, as they are the expert everyone else needs to listen to. If that means that you need the school janitor to sit in on meetings when you are deciding how to use donated space in the school for your project, you need to listen to what he has to say... who knows the ins and outs of a facility better than the person who must maintain it?

If you are planning a fund raiser such as a walkathon, who knows better than a participant if the route they trod in a previous walk is really good?

The trick is to establish a mindset that says, "We will carefully consider who really has the information, expertise and insight to speak to each aspect of our effort, invite them to help in the planning and then LISTEN to what they have to say.... REGARDLESS OF THEIR TITLE, POSITION OR ASSUMPTIONS ON OUR PART."

It is a willingness to establish a climate that identifies and values diversity and perspectives and will honor these diversities in a person when we come to their area of expertise. This is the spirit of Leadershift.

Now think about that. That sounds so democratic, so logical, but how many times have you sat in planning meetings where incredible decisions were made WITHOUT the perspective of the persons most intimately involved? I'll bet you've even been part of "recruitment" sessions where someone's name came up, everyone agreed they would be perfect for the job, but everyone also agreed that "they're too busy; they wouldn't have time for this". A decision made without even asking the person themselves!

In Leadershift, there is a willingness to gather anyone most involved and allow the leader role to be passed to them when it comes time to discuss their perspective.

The ultimate leader continues in her or his role of guiding and moving the process, but is grateful to step into the shadows and watch others take the lead for a time.

Leader-shift; shifting-leadership: a time to let a lot of good people contribute to the success of the effort, have their very own 15 minutes of celebrity, and, at the realization of the vision, possibly even a standing ovation! (3-4)

How wonderful, and how much stronger and effective the effort.

Characteristic #2:"**Don't Fence Me In**"

Leadershift also means that you embrace what General Electric, in their 1994 Annual Report, calls "Boundaryless Behavior". This is defined as the removal of walls and layers that separate people and inhibit creativity and innovation.

Such walls, GE stated, "cramp people, inhibit creativity, waste time, restrict vision, smother dreams, and above all, slow things down. The challenge is to chip away at and eventually break down these walls and barriers, both among ourselves and between ourselves and the outside world."

It's a great concept, and one critical to Leadershift, as it allows people to stop thinking of themselves in a separate, walled-off section of an organization, and instead, see themselves as part of the whole. For a volunteer program, that means that instead of seeing itself as one of a dozen departments in a large organization which must compete with the others for resources and attention, it sees its role as being a part of all departments.(3-5)

This is integration at its most basic level. It steps outside any perfectly drawn lines that forbid it to wander "where it doesn't belong" or "outside its place" and instead, is open to becoming part of any area where volunteers might serve needs. It also refers to information, which is (let's face it) power.(3-6)

The greatest task before you in adopting Leadershift's philosophy of no boundaries, may be piercing the walls of long-standing fiefdoms and empires where those at the helm hold information or control that others do not have.

If you have ever tried to turn an ingrained auxiliary in a new direction in partnership with non-volunteers, you know what I'm talking about. They resist, hold back and throw obstacles in your path to prove "it just won't work!" (3-7)

If you've ever tried to change a project begun by a founder, you may have seen them change from a benign mentor into a predatory beast with your throat their noon meal! And if you have even dared to suggest a change in the procedure or format of an accounting nightmare, I'll hope that the hair singed off your head from the resulting blast of "How DARE you!" has grown back by now.

It's not easy to break down barriers or to chip away at those sacred boxes on a management chart, but Leadershift demands it. If you cannot accomplish that in the larger organization in which your volunteer program exists, let it go and simply model boundaryless behavior within your realm of leadership. Then work to integrate volunteers throughout the total organization so that instead of seeing volunteers corralled in an isolated corner, people begin to see volunteers as a critical part of all aspects of service delivery. Who knows, even the Accounting Department may see the value in gaining the expertise of a retired CPA volunteer and let them alter a form or two! (3-8)

Characteristic #3: "Let's Win One for the Gipper!"

Leadershift requires that you work more and more into the role of Coach.

Coaching paid staff who will directly supervise volunteers; coaching volunteers on how to work with paid staff and to whom to go when problems arise (usually the direct supervisor, not the volunteer administrator); coaching everyone on how speak on behalf of the agency's work when they are out in the community, getting names of those interested and bringing them back to the volunteer program office, etc. (3-9)

You may need to coach people in specific skills such as public speaking, risk management, reporting, interviewing, recruiting, etc. Coaching has so many variances that it will probably become second nature to you, and you will slip in and out of this role dozens of times a day.

Understand that the value of coaching is that it's opposite is doing the task yourself. When you coach others for action, you do not have to take that action yourself. It is really a subtle form of delegation, where, for example, you show others how to write a story for the local newspaper rather than your having to do it.

The coaching role differs from the strict definition of delegation in that it also may require some cheer leading from the sideline.....helping people believe in their own new-found ability to accomplish a task....encouraging teams working on a problem so that they have the confidence to carry on.

It also requires a healthy and mature sense of self that does NOT require a constant feeding of ego. Good coaches let the spotlight center on the people who score the points; they do not need to have it fall on themselves. When on-lookers give a standing ovation to the team of volunteers and paid staff who worked two months to meet a particularly difficult challenge in the agency, the good Coach feels pride in having played a part in empowering the team, but no jealousy at being part of the applauders rather than the applauded. Think about that. Being a Coach may mean you are always in the shadows; if that is disturbing to you, you may want to confront your own needs and see where they might best be met. (3-10)

Characteristic #4: "Let It Go, Let It Go, Let It Go......"

Another characteristic of anyone adopting Leadershift, is the ability to let go of things. As a Coach you would need to let go of a need for the spotlight. In other aspects you would need to let go of getting credit for works you may initiate but not actually do; of ideas picked up by others and even labeled as their own; and often of good ideas that are rejected by those in authority.

There are times when letting go is hard. That good idea I spoke of, for example, may be hard to put aside, especially when you can clearly see its wisdom. It's hard to be a Columbus who sees round when everyone around you sees flat. (3-11)

Decide when it is best to let go of something and when it's time to stand your ground and fight for what you believe in. If you decide to let go, simply file your idea away for another time and place...the idea is probably still good, it's simply the wrong timing.

If you are slighted in some way, do what you can to untangle any misinformation, and then let it go. If you have a dispute with someone you must work with, do what you can to settle the difference, even if that's agreeing to disagree, and move on. Let it go.

You'll know by the hair on the back of your neck if the subject is one that cannot be let go.....those things usually surrounding ethics, values and mission. Remember that Leadershift means that you can take different positions as circumstances change, but when you can see that letting go is for the greater good, do so.(3-12)

Gunny-sacking grievances, past hurts, slights of long ago and other such baggage will eventually weigh you down and explode at improper times! When wounded, either confront the aggressor and settle the matter or walk away and let it go. (3-13)

Characteristic #5: Establishing the Vision

Here's that vision thing again.

The volunteer program executive MUST own the vision of the organization and her specific department so that she can share it with everyone else. The principle of Leadershift requires that she have the flexibility to be able to describe it to the variety of others she will meet in ways that they will be able to understand. (3-14)

Let's say that you are the leader of a teen pregnancy program whose vision is to help pregnant teens cope with their pregnancy and also to impact the question of children having children in the general population.

When speaking with educators, your description of the vision would focus on helping teens finish high school in order to be better equipped to support a child and to be part of a program of peer counseling and education that helps classmates avoid pregnancy while in school.

When talking to medical personnel, your description of the goal of your program would lean toward the benefits that would come as pregnant teens learned pre-natal care, well-baby techniques and how to cope with a child in order to prevent future child abuse.

Even though the vision remains the same, you as leader are shifting how you describe it so that the listener gets a clear picture of the vision, especially from the perspective that interests them the most.

What you are doing, in marketing terms, is tailoring your appeal, a legitimate strategy designed to establish a relationship with others and make your vision "real" to them.

You must also keep the vision alive for the people already within your program. Here are some suggestions for just that:

1. Make sure in the interviewing, placing and orientation processes that the vision is clearly articulated and feedback is extracted from recruits to insure that she or he has "gotten it". Introduce multiple ways to project the vision and to check to see that it has been understood. This is not always easy.

2. State the vision in terms of people helped. If you have clients, picture the good outcome of your services in photographs and other visual forms (graphs, statistics, etc.). If you lead a program from the arts, for example, that has a more difficult time identifying "clients", brainstorm with others as to how you will depict your efforts as it effects people..... wide-eyed children enjoying a museum; satisfied adults looking enriched as they view art work.

3. If your program addresses a critical need, find a way to graphically show this need. Have the resulting photos or symbols at work stations around your site, so that people are reminded constantly of why they are working so hard and who they are working for. Change photos regularly so that they are noticed and create on-going interest.

4. When recognizing volunteers and staff for their work, think of ways that clients can be part of the recognition. When I was National Director for Project Concern International, a charity that helped the children of poverty, some of the most prized gifts were drawings by our small clients in our hospitals around the world. Another cherished gift was a bracelet worn by the Vietnamese Montengard tribal members that was given to staff. Such gifts symbolize the relationship of helper and helped and typically has great meaning to the former.

Keep in mind that people work for people and that a continuing theme of volunteers (and dedicated paid staff) in studying their motivation for working is often "making a difference". By keeping the vision alive and visible to everyone, you are reminding them of why they are there, what they are really trying to accomplish and offering the strength they may need to carry out difficult assignments.

Remember also that in helping to keep the vision alive for others you are keeping it uppermost for yourself too, a factor that may get YOU through some dark hours!

Besides a well-defined vision being a motivator, it is also an evaluation tool against which you can measure the actions of your program. As you evaluate efforts or design new programs, use the vision as a yardstick by asking:

"Is what we do (or plan to do) going to help us achieve our vision? Is it compatible with our mission? Is it congruent with our dream and primary aspiration?"

If any of the answers to that bank of questions is "no", you may need to rethink your plans or activities. If it does not "fit" with your mission, why do it? A lot of groups, in doing this exercise of measuring everything against the mission or vision, have weeded out a great deal of extraneous work and therefore, been able to refocus worker's energies on truly pertinent efforts.

Sometimes measuring congruency of efforts against the mission statement or vision of a program can be downright embarrassing, by the way. Take for example the group that decided to collect household furnishings for the homeless. After successfully gathering two garages full of stuff it dawned on them that homeless people have no where to put such items. They too could have used Gilda Radner's admonition of "Oh.....Never mind".

As to keeping the vision in clear perspective and in front of everyone, the decree must be:

"Always mind."

Characteristic #6: **Quality and the TQM Bug**

TQM is the buzzword of today. Standing for "Total Quality Management" it is the brainchild of C. Edwards Demming, who tried to offer it to American manufacturers after World War II and was laughed out of the country.......straight into the arms of Japanese business leaders who saw the wisdom of his words, convinced him to teach everyone there who lead any kind of effort and made him Mr. Number One as they saw his theories work.

I see no need to detail Japan's rise to post-World War II dominance in world markets, but I do find it ironic that in my childhood in the 1940's "Made in Japan" meant something had little or no quality and then in my early adult years in the 1960's, it came to mean exactly the opposite.

Other writers and teachers besides Demming preach quality.... Tom Peters, Lee Iacocca, Peter Drucker...etc. Each suggests his own way of bringing quality to your program. Together they offer you a smorgasbord of ideas from which you can select.

The point here is not to enumerate every quality management theory or process, but to reinforce what I'm sure you already, innately understand about Leadershift:

"Attention to quality must be part of every design, procedure, effort and delivery of the service outlined by the vision."

Bringing quality to a program means:

1. Providing top quality services to clients; often exceeding their expectations.

2. Treating each customer (client) with individual concern for their needs.

3. Giving services as quickly as possible and quicker than any competition.

4. Eliminating wasted time, cost, energy and/or material as you deliver services.

5. Insuring any products offered by your program are top notch & worth the cost.

6. Treating everyone within the organization like a customer: with concern & caring.

7. Constantly measuring results against the mission. Did it do what was intended?

8. Constantly stimulating (and rewarding) suggestions for improvement.

9. Allowing no sacred cows; everything must be eligible for review and improvement.

10. Bringing people together who impact or are impacted by a process and having them work to insure quality and constantly seek improvement.

11. Involving outside suppliers and other constituents in the process.

12. Making everyone involved feel responsible, proud, and rewarded for their efforts.

To bring the concern about quality into the minds of paid and volunteer staff alike, introduce it in orientations, trainings, newsletters, bulletin boards and every other vehicle you can capture. (3-15) Ford automobiles improved markedly when the leaders of that company created the slogan, "Quality is Job One!". Much of the improvement is credited to the fact that everywhere workers, buyers, and potential customers turned, that slogan was in front of them!

In TV ads you saw the actual factory workers not only putting their part of the Ford onto the assembly-line body, but sometimes *signing* it....and thereby using the most powerful tool of personal responsibility.... one's own name!

Leadershift attitudes create the arena that encourages constant reflection, assessment and re-tooling of efforts to make them more efficient and effective. Change is not seen as a condemnation of what was but a striving for the best possible quality in everything being done. What was before is not seen as bad or poor, but as a stair step that serves as a foundation for more stairs to come in the upward climb toward top quality.

Leaders of today's volunteer programs keep this in their own mind and insure that everyone else see this same vision, making quality and customer satisfaction "job one" for them too!

Characteristic #7: "The Gull Sees Farthest...."

In Richard Bach's wonderful little book jammed with lessons of life, Jonathon Livingston Seagull is being coached by Fletcher, his flight instructor. They are discussing the benefits of flying higher than everyone else, setting standards for others and having the clearest vision. The great line that brings wisdom to the effort states:

"The gull sees farthest, who flies highest."

That may seem a round-about way to introduce a critical characteristic of Leadershift that deals with the need for you as leader to set high ethical standards and values. As we examine it together, however, I hope you'll see why that quote symbolizes what needs to be said on this subject.

First, the leader is the one out front who is being watched by followers all the time. Leaders set the pace and others copy it so as to "keep in step". What they do and how they do it becomes the pattern that is repeated by those who are being led, with the leader's attitude flowing through the ranks of all workers.

If you have ever had to work in an organization whose leaders were negative, abusive and over-controlling, you know that that attitude contaminated everything and everyone involved no matter where they stood on the management chart. If, on the other hand, you were fortunate enough to work in a program led by caring, creative, open leaders, you know also that THAT attitude permeated the whole effort.

Understanding this will help you to think carefully about the ethical standards and values you not only want to talk about, but also model and project through actions and attitudes. Those projections determine the values within your program, and set the parameters for actions by others.

Take time to think about ethics and values in your organization. Draw together others to discuss this issue and create a list of values that you will project to volunteers and paid staff with which you work. Brainstorm ways to reward those who exemplify those values and ways to deal with those who do not. Identify those ethical behaviors that are non-negotiable and MUST be adhered to at all times and the consequences for those people who do not follow them. Realize that you will need the input of the administration when drawing up your list of non-negotiables that might include:

1. Never revealing confidential information.

2. Never misappropriating funds or resources.

3. Never putting a client in harms way.

4. Never mistreating a client, customer, co-worker or colleague.

5. Never giving dis-information (wrong information given knowingly).

The list may go on for your program, but that's a start.

You may also want to list those things which are highly valued and therefore dictate behavior:

1. Being on time.

2. Showing up for work when promised.

3. Being honest and forthright.

4. Communicating openly, not hiding information.

5. Valuing others around you.

6. Accepting diversity; seeing others as people, not categories.

7. Avoiding assumptions; getting the facts.

8. Being kind.

      C. 1996 S. Vineyard. STOP MANAGING VOLUNTEERS!

9. Avoiding little "power-towers": those fiefdoms ruled by people who believe that because they have been around so long they have all the answers and everyone must bow to their will. Phooey.

Again, your list will be much longer, but this is a beginning. This list will also begin to identify "norms" which are the unwritten rules that govern a group. These are discussed in greater detail in Chapter Twelve.

The demand for ethical behavior is a cry the general population has clearly offered, as seen in trends analysis by such famous researchers as John Naisbitt, Patricia Aburdene ("Megatrends", "Megatrends 2000", etc.), Peter Drucker ("The New Realities") and Faith Popcorn ("The Popcorn Report").

As leaders we need to demonstrate by words and actions the most ethical behavior and positive values, so that anyone scrutinizing us will find the highest levels of ethical behavior and vision.

Indeed, the one who flies highest does indeed see furthest.

Characteristic #8: **Getting Out of the Way....**

In Leadershift one has to have quick mobility...sometimes of the feet, sometimes of the mouth and always of the attitude.

The good leader knows when to walk beside a person, when to coax, when to coach, when to cheer and most importantly, when to get out of the way and let them go on their own. (3-16)

We are in an age when mentoring has become popular. As I've watched this trend through a decade or more, I've become alarmed that the wonderful concept of mentoring (bringing someone along; helping them to a greater potential, etc.) gets lost because too many mentors forget to get out of the way. Some stay too long because they have not recognized that their mentee is ready to be on their own; others, tragically, realize that their pupil may outshine them and therefore stay close in order to retain control and predominance.

In Leadershift, the wise leader may adopt the mentor role and all that is good about it, but shifts away at the first sign that the pupil is ready or desirous of going it alone. They also stand ready to jump back in when invited or to assist in preventing disasters that will effect the overall mission of the organization. Learning from mistakes is fine, but not at the total expense of the effort.

Learn to read the signs of when those you are coaching or mentoring will be strengthened by your NOT being at their right hand. See this "letting go" as part of your teaching.....much as a good teacher lets her pupil practice-teach, work in the lab or do an independent study on their own, with progress reviews as needed.

Watch also for times when you sense that your presence (in group work, for example) is inhibiting the independence and creative thinking of those around you.

To detect this, watch for:

1. Eyes turning to you when a question or problem is posed.

2. Silence by everyone that is in deference to your presence.

3. People trying to respond to an issue who punctuate their remarks with comments to you. ("Here's what I think, but of course you, Boss, might not like that....")

4. Everyone referring to what has already been done, especially by you.

5. People whose body language tells you they have something to say but are holding back.

6. The hair on the back of your neck is telling you it would be better if you left!

That last item is not a flippant comment. I really do urge you in all matters to listen to your intuition and body for signals that something is going on. Trust your instincts. Trust your perceptions and that illusive sixth sense we often have but ignore.

Remember that Columbus was right in thinking round even though everyone else was thinking flat!

Characteristic #9:
When Inviting Everyone Into the Pool, Remember That Not All Can Swim!

When accepting Leadershift as your "management style", keep in mind that primarily it is dealing in human BEINGS, and only subsequently human-DOINGS.

That means that there are certain premises you must have firmly imbedded in your belief system about people:

1. People want to succeed. They do not come to you to fail.

2. Most people are honest and well-meaning. Always assess intention when confronted with problems; their intentions may have been good but their actions poor.

3. People's greatest need is to be cared about (not *for;* about).

4. Listen carefully to what people are saying; hear between the lines. Care about what they are saying.

5. Believe in people's genuine commitment; don't get hung up on their ability to explain WHY they care, just accept it.

6. Understand that people change; the volunteer that came to you six months ago may already be a different person.

7. Assume the positive; change the assumption only after being proven wrong.

8. People are never stereotypical of any classification; see folks as individuals.

9. Everyone has something to teach us; look for learning opportunities.

10. People are usually the most competent when given a task they love and that matters; expect competence.

11. People live up or down to your expectations.

12. People give you more of what you recognize and reward; less of what you ignore.

13. People really do have a whole other life outside your agency; they are not totally defined by their involvement with you. Give them space.

14. People are good; especially when you believe in them. Do so.

15. Focus on people's capacities rather than their capacities.

16. Keep clear that the *being* of a person is their essence, not what they *do* or the title they hold. Don't define people by their work; this is too narrow when measuring their worth.

And lastly, keep in mind that for some...a very few, I would predict...at least one of the above is not true. There are dishonest people; some people are not well-intentioned; some cannot be competent in what you need to have done; some do not really have any life outside their work with you.....etc. etc.

There are those folks who simply will not fit your agency and its mission. Let go of the idea that your secondary mission is to include, fix, save and rework everyone that comes through your door. Forget the idea that your volunteers are also your clients and that you are responsible for their entire life.

Even let go of the idea that everyone can and would benefit from working under a Leadershift style of management. Some volunteers want to be managed directly by the leader and anything less smacks in their mind of rejection and dismissal.

I know several volunteer program leaders to whom Leadershift seems like a foreign language they do not plan to learn because it wouldn't work in their situation. That's OK. No one style is for everyone.... leader or follower.

Create what works for you, the assignments you have on your desk, and the work to be done at specific times with specific people. The goal is to accomplish the mission of your organization and be true to the vision. If Leadershift won't get you there, take the trolley that will!

And that's the beauty I see in Leadershift, even it understands that not everyone can embrace its' philosophy. "Everyone in the pool" is an invitation, not a mandate..... especially to those of us who cannot or do not choose to swim.

Characteristic #10: **Planning Your Retirement**

Excuse me? That's miles away......

Not really.

Whether you have been on the job one day, one year or 41, I hope you will begin to plan for your retirement immediately. I say this after 15 years of working with groups around the world and seeing an epidemic that goes unrecognized and has no fund raisers planned to stem its tide:

"SupeLeader-Leftism"

Leadershift has many components as we have looked at in this chapter. It's most critical characteristic, if it is to indeed create strong programs, is that it must be true to its own wording: Leader-**shift**.

The single most deadly thing I see that can kill the best of programs, is that a strong leader leaves and though the program struts along for a short period under a new leader, it soon begins to stagger because so much of what the program WAS was intertwined with the leader herself. (3-17)

Typically the outstanding programs hire someone to follow a charismatic leader's departure who is a personal favorite of the Board. Often they appoint a person who has admired the program and all the accolades and looks at it as so self-sustaining that little work will have to go into leading it.

This second person comes in, rides on the wave of success generated in the past, but then begins to run into trouble as key people move out, new problems arise and old solutions won't work.

The problem is that others around the program, seeing only the outer crust of what is happening, do not see how hard the original leader was working beneath the surface to bring about the seemingly effortless and highly successful results.

The only way I can think of to solve this malady, is for every volunteer program administrator to begin to plan for their own retirement from day one; creating systems that will outlast their presence; developing leadership to follow them; insuring that people do not become dependent on them for results.

In doing so, you may be giving your program the greatest gift of all: wings on which to fly on its own, independent and internally strong.

You will be giving the people involved in your program the truest definition of Leadershift.... the ability to lead through many shifts in leadership; to stay strong because of and in spite of change.

It is the ultimate example of letting go, getting out of the way, ethical behavior, empowering the vision, insuring on-going quality, extending boundaryless behavior, coaching, and inspiring leadership shifts for effective work teams.

Leadershift.....like most of life, it is what you make of it.

The Great Idea Heist

There are many management strategists who develop a theory, apply it to corporate America, find success and expand on this in a book, lectures and consultations. In many such theories that come along, we can find a grain of wisdom that can be adapted to our needs in volunteer administration. Because these ideas are so abundant, its easy to forget what you may have picked up as the theories flew through your consciousness!

Use this worksheet to jot down the "ah-has!" you get as you read about the latest management trick of the day. I'll start you off with an admonition from Tom Peters, co-author of *In Search of Excellence:*

☼ 'Spend time and money to thoroughly train those employees whom customers first encounter. Give them the authority to solve problems.'

☞ Adaptation: Avoid assigning new volunteers as telephone answers or reception-desk personnel. Instead, place very experienced volunteers in these jobs who know the organization thoroughly and have been trained for outstanding phone & reception skills. Insure that they are trained in clear, concise communication & problem solving. Clearly define their authority and parameters. Keep them up-to-date on changing information they might need. Give them the authority & information to solve problems.

Leadershift Roles

Coach	Consultant	Researcher
Boss	Power Broker	Coordinator
Advisor	Absentee Ruler	Inspiration
Doer	Cheerleader	Teacher
Expert	Technician	Networker
Peace maker	Conflict Solver	Referee
Score Keeper	Rule Maker	Task-master
Arbitrator	Visionary	Clan-gatherer
Team Builder	Reflector	Traffic Cop
Reminder	Clarifier	Norm-enforcer
Norm-setter	Thanks-giver	Listener
Counselor	Interpreter	Watch Dog
Empowerer	Challenger	Cool Cat
Disciplinarian	Fun-seeker	Communicator
Planner	Trainer	Role-model
Definer	Leader	Follower
Warrior-Defender	Learner	Change Agent
Advocate	Manager	Administrator
Executive	Visionary	Servant
Volunteer	Volunteer	Volunteer

What other roles are unique to you as you respond to the demands of your job?

The Ultimate Leader

It is critical, for every effort in which you are involved, to identify the "ultimate leader"; the person who takes over-all responsibility for a goal or activity. This assumes that the buck always stops on your desk for final accountability for everything that goes on in your setting that involves volunteers, BUT, here I want you to identify the ultimate leader who has taken responsibility for a particular effort.

Project or Goal:

Ultimate Leader:

Leaders who take responsibility for various parts of this effort: (This is critical to clarify; these people are ultimate-leaders for smaller parts of the whole.)

If you see yourself as ultimate leader of every project, be careful... you may need to shift some of this leadership role to others so that you are not carrying all the load of your department. Good leaders understand that people feel most invested when they take responsibility for activities. Let go of a need for infinite control of every detail of work; you may feel always being the ultimate leader insures "perfection" but it rarely does and can discourage strong others who resent never being allowed to truly lead. Carefully examine your attitude toward delegation and watch out for burnout!

c. 1996. Sue Vineyard. Stop Managing Volunteers!

Passing the Leader's Baton

1. Think of a forth-coming project. Describe it in a few words:

2. Who needs to be involved in its planning and implementation?

3. Why do you need each person listed above? (Skills, contacts, perspective, etc.)

4. How will you empower each to do their job and when the team gathers, get this person to act as leader as they describe their activities?

5. Think through what role you will play as these others lead:

A Relational Over-view of Your Organization

This worksheet is designed to help you look at all the various parts of your agency or organization and your relationships to each. As this will change constantly, you will need to update information. Hopefully, this overview will help you see where your support already lies and where more needs to be developed.

Using photocopies of this worksheet, list all the various departments in your agency. Keep each sheet in your file for reference, revisions, etc.

Updated: _____

Department:_____Responsibilities:_____

Lead by:_____Other staff:_____

How do you relate to this department? (what do you give to or take from them?)

Are you dependent on this department?   For what?

Is this department dependent on you?   For what?

What is your professional relationship with its leader? Staff?

Do volunteers now work in this department?   How many?
Doing what?   Supervised by whom?

Do you see any barriers to harmonious interactions? How might they be removed?

What systems must you use to interact? Are they simple & direct? If not, how can they be changed?

What needs might this department have that you could fill in the future? How might you accomplish the integration of volunteers into such needs?

Who Has Information?

If we are to be effective we must have the information we need to do our work. Use this worksheet over and over in tracking information sources and strategies to gain access to the data you need.

....

Project:

_____

Information Needed:	by(date)	Best Sources	How to gather:

Obstacles

Anticipate possible obstacles (without causing them to become self-fulfilling prophesies!) so that you can strategize paths around them:

Project: Goal:

Who has a vested interest in this effort?

Will this projects' inception replace or alter a previous effort? Which? How?

Who were key players in the older efforts? If still involved, what are their positions on the new effort?

What possible objections might arise as you work on this new project? How can you reduce or eliminate these objections?

What strategies can you devise to circumvent or evaporate any barriers to the successful completion of this project? What key supporters do you need to help you and how can you enlist them?

Boundaryless Vision

What is your vision of how volunteers could enhance your entire organization if they were allow to do so?

Keep this vision statement handy to remind yourself of possibilities and to refresh your spirit on darker days!

Coaching Others

What paid staff will be directly supervising volunteers? How will you prepare these people to work most productively with volunteers?

Paid staff supervising volunteers:

...What can you do to insure staff has a positive attitude toward volunteers?

...How can you insure clear job designs are created and understood?

...What specific skills must you coach staff on as they work with volunteers?

...What systems have you devised for staff to report concerns or needs?

...If problems arise, how are they going to be handled? By whom?

...What expectations do staff have concerning volunteers? Are they realistic? How can you insure they are realistic?

Feeling Good While Letting Go

When you coach others to accomplish goals rather than doing them yourself, it requires that you step back and let others shine. It also means that your own feelings of satisfaction must come by less direct involvement.

It may help you in this subtle transition to identify your own needs for satisfaction:

I feel most satisfied at work when........

I feel energized when...............

I'm really proud of....................

It's important that the following people know what I've accomplished: (examine why also)

When to Hold and When to Fold!

Creative volunteer program leaders typically have many ideas swirling around in their heads. The wiser ones know that timing is everything and that even the best ideas, if presented at the wrong timing, can be shot down. Use this worksheet to help you select the best timing for your own ideas.

Idea:

Who needs to be involved? What would their stake or reward be?

What other demands do these people need to juggle as they consider involvement in your idea?

What timing might be best for the presentation of this idea? Why?

How can it best be presented (in writing, formal verbal presentation, informal conversation, in detail or outlined, etc.):

What preparations can you make to enhance your chances of this idea's acceptance?

If it is better to defer this idea until later, what can you do to set the stage for its later presentation? What needs to be in place for this idea to be seen favorably? Can you influence such factors? How?

Drawing the Line

Everyone has some issues that cannot be compromised: values, ethics, basic beliefs, etc. It may be helpful for you to list your personal and professional "non-negotiables" in order to fortify your resolve when faced with conflicting demands.

My deepest values include...............

The most important things, issues or people in my life are..........

I will not compromise..................

All of the same questions above apply to your organization. There are non-negotiable values, ethics and standards as well as highly valued behaviors. List them:

Prescription for Unresolved Issues

Holding on to past grievances can only contaminate current efforts. Clean out past hurts as best you can. Here's a bit of help:

I still feel anger/hurt/pain/discomfort about the following:

The people I hold responsible for each of the above are:

When did each happen:

Two options I have for resolving each are:

     #1: Confronting those responsible to resolve the issue.
     #2: Letting it go; filing it under "Experience" and stopping my negative reaction to it.

Which will I choose for each grievance listed above? How will I do each?

What can I learn from each experience? What good came out of each?

Remember that you control your reactions to what happens. Choose resolution & let it go.

c. 1996. Sue Vineyard. Stop Managing Volunteers!

That Vision Thing

State the vision or mission of your organization in as few words as possible:

State the vision or mission of your department in as few words as possible:

How can these visions be best expressed to others?

Staff:

Volunteers:

Hierarchy:

Clients:

Public:

Supporters:

Others:

Quality

How can you build a continual commitment to quality into your efforts among:

Volunteers:

Paid Staff:

What quality standards exist for your programs?

How do you plan to review activities to check on quality? What reflection efforts do you plan. How can you capture ideas that could enhance quality?

Mentoring

A critical role fostered by Leadershift is that of mentoring... helping to develop future leaders. To keep this task in the forefront of your thinking, it may be helpful to sketch out real efforts to encourage and empower others. (You may want to photocopy this worksheet in order to have one per person for their confidential file.)

Potential future leaders and their specific strengths:

For each, check those area of experience they are accumulating. When they lack experience in any area, consider options you have to assist them in gaining needed experiences:

....

Skill Area	Dates	Assignment Remarks	How I might help;

....

Managing Volunteers

Working w/Staff

Administrative:
...budget:
...reporting
...risk mangmt.
...planning
...systems

Training

Evaluating

Public Relations

Marketing

Recognition

Event Planning

Problem Solving

Negotiating

Motivating

Collaborating

....

Other:

General Comments:

Moving On

Too many excellent programs fall apart after the strong leader departs. Incorporate into your efforts strategies to insure that what you are building up during your tenure is carried on. Mentoring others (3-16) is a start; here are others you can consider:

What innovations have begun under my leadership?

Which came about because of specific skills/experiences/knowledge unique to me?

What steps can I take now to pass these skills etc. on to others?

What can I do now to insure that efforts under my leadership are NOT dependent on my presence?

Who would make the decision to hire my replacement?

How can I impact that decision?

(No one ever has to see this, so be truthful; don't be shy about listing your accomplishments.)

Chapter Four

Thinking Entrepreneurially

The American Heritage Dictionary states that the definition of an entrepreneur is:

"A person who organizes, operates and assumes the risk for a business enterprise".

In our modern day use of the term it has also come to mean one who is creative and so dedicated to a vision that they will devise innovative ways to reach their objective; they are uninhibited by anyone else's definition of what "should" be and daring enough to create their own pathway toward their vision.

The volunteer program leader who stretches outside the boundaries of traditional "volunteer management" is reaching toward a new competency, assuming the posture of an entrepreneur; taking risks, thinking innovatively and creating new ways to achieve that all important vision.

I believe that this unique competency will actually, in time, become the norm among strong programs across North America and be mimicked internationally as more and more countries turn through democratization toward innovative ways to create a voluntary sector in their nations.

Going Outside The Lines

The thing that strikes me whenever I encounter an entrepreneurial program leader is the number of times they defy tradition, refuse to believe "it can't be done" and basically create their own design outside defined lines drawn before.

One such genius said she simply put on her most innocent look after a bold new action and replied to those who said, "But we never".... "Gosh, I didn't know we couldn't." Because she was always guided by ethical behavior and felt there was a better way to accomplish her goal than what had been done for decades, she proceeded on a new course by forging ahead, not asking permission (which she knew would be denied) and offering her "apology" afterwards.

Another volunteer administrator used a similar approach by going ahead with what she felt would be a less complicated and more effective method of recruiting new people to her organization. When she realized great success and her supervisor found out how she had done it, she was met with a comment that became her invitation to continue innovating: "We never thought of doing it that way! How could we have been so blind? Keep it up."

Every time you do take a step "outside the lines" of conventional behavior in an organization, you are taking a risk. Risk that others will be angered, risk of failure, risk of treading on territory others think solely belongs to them. At each venture only you can assess the wisdom and risk factors of your action. Sometimes you may decide that it is worth the risk and feel certain enough of its success that you will dare to go ahead. (4-1)

At other times you may sense that although you believe in the validity of what you want to do, you feel that the timing is all wrong, and choose to delay it.

It is a given that the more successful the outcome, the more likely you are to receive "forgiveness" for ignoring set patterns, or sometimes, as in the one case above, praise for your creativity. Keep in mind however, that if it fails or if your success is seen by some as a threat to their own territory or reputation, you may have to dodge a few slings and arrows.

When assessing how and when to proceed innovatively, you might consider:

1. What is it that I want to accomplish?

2. What will be better if this is done successfully?

3. Why must I ignore the traditional to accomplish this?

4. Who will be effected by the accomplishment? How? Who needs to be involved?

5. Who might object to the new process I plan to take? How? Why? Can we afford their displeasure?

6. Who might be hurt by the process or the success of this effort?

7. What might be their reaction?

8. What harm might they do me if their reaction is anger or feeling threatened?

9. Is there anything I can do to blunt a negative reaction from others? What?

10. Is the timing right? If not now, when? Why? Can I "sell" the idea?

11. If this fails, what would be the consequences?

12. If this fails or succeeds, what will the cost to me and my department be?

13. Is the cost worth the risk? Would it be worth it if it fails? Succeeds?

14. If the answers to the above questions are "yes"", it's time to begin.

I would then urge you to diagram the new procedure you plan to take and run it by a trusted other to see if you have overlooked anything and if your plan can be easily explained to others.

Often we create something that is very clear to us because we have lived with it and it came from our own thinking. In trying to explain it to others, however, we discover that a great deal of background thinking has to be offered before they can truly "see" its wisdom.

If that is the case, go back and hone it to the point that it can be clearly explained in no more than a few minutes....five at the most. Put it on paper in the simplest of forms to reinforce your explanation and try it out again on trusted others to insure its clarity.

Rehearse mentally how it will be carried out. Think about worst-case scenarios and even rehearse your contingency plans for those, so that when implementation comes, you will be prepared for almost anything that happens.

To think like an entrepreneur, you must first accept the risks you will be taking and the price they will demand, but then push ahead with your plans, believe in your own instincts and create new and innovative pathways for your efforts that will help you attain your vision.

Customer servive

During the depression in the early 1930's, my mother was fortunate to have a job at Marshall Field's department store in Chicago. For years it was that town's flagship store, the one that people across the country knew about because of it's reputation as one of our nation's finest.

Every possible item you could think of could be found on its seven floors, and Mom was very proud to be part of the "Field's family" as she sold the finest pots and pans of the day! I was especially impressed by what she told me was the one thing every Fields clerk had to keep uppermost in their mind:

"If we do not have what the customer wants, we will find it for them. If the customer is dissatisfied, return their money. Do whatever the customer asks, because THE CUSTOMER IS ALWAYS RIGHT."

Recently Tom Peters wrote in his column about a hotel in Washington, DC whose front-desk person was unable to make the simple decision of allowing him to check into a room early and then allowing him to stay in that same room for the night.

The clerk kept insisting that he would have to come back down to the front desk, luggage in hand, after 3 PM to be reassigned to a different room for the night. He was paying for the extra day rate for the two hours he needed in the afternoon, and had a confirmed reservation for the night, but because the clerk was not able to make the decision herself to allow Peters to keep the same room, he would have the inconvenience of returning to the lobby to check out of one room and into another.

When I read that, and Peter's call to authorize the people on the front lines of service to make decisions that serve the needs of the customer, I was reminded of the Marshall Field's policy drummed into my mother that every clerk was authorized, even commanded, to do anything to satisfy the customer because the underlying philosophy was that "the customer is always right."

Years later....in the 1970's..... I spoke with the mother of a dear friend who worked at Fields in their customer service center. She confirmed that the philosophy remained the same and that she and her coworkers looked forward to every Valentine's Day and New Years when they heard from the same customer year after year. The story was always identical: at Valentine's Day the customer returned a 90% consumed box of Frango mint candy saying it did not taste good and she wanted a refund; the week after New Years she always returned a sterling silver punch bowl and 24 matching cups she had "bought" the week before and charged to her account. She was, of course, unhappy with the set and was returning it for full credit.

She got her refund and her credit every year, because, as my friend's mother put it, "The customer is always right!....no matter what."

There are great lessons in these stories for the volunteer program leader. Think about your own applications and add them to the following list of learnings:

1. **Empower** those front line volunteers and paid staff to make decisions to meet needs.(4-2)

2. Give them the **information** they need to accommodate changing needs.

3. **Outline those actions** which are **NOT acceptable** to adopt. To give examples: in a health care facility, it would not be acceptable to allow a patient or visitor to wander in to certain areas of the building that are off-limits to outsiders; it would also not be permissible for a volunteer to respond to a patient's unusual request without checking with the nurse.

4. Never deny common-sense service, especially to a famous columnist!

Customer service is more of an *attitude* than anything. Establish a spirit of helpfulness among those you oversee that they can carry on to the clients or customers your program serves. Treat those who work under your auspices as if they were customers, being responsive to their needs and wants, listening carefully and being both polite and kind, and you will most likely find that they will model this same behavior with those they encounter.

Customer service finds much of its success by identifying and *anticipating what needs* clients or customers might have so that everyone who will interact with them can be prepared with appropriate procedures and responses. (4-3)

When designing customer service within your organization, be sure to look at both the systems side and the people side of the issue. Procedures outline how customers will be served; people will determine how the services are delivered.

Customer service, always within the bounds of reason and safety, is the art of making every "customer" (internal and external) feel human, unique, valued and the object of total attention and caring. It is *responsiveness to needs*, even if that response is a "no", because of a greater good.

As Tom Peters, in his Aug. 15, 1994 Chicago Tribune column concluded:

> *"Business success..... only comes from turning every front-line employee into a one-person entrepreneurial enterprise that happens to be embedded in a much larger corporate body."*

When challenged on this statement by one manager who demanded to know how to insure consistency, Peters replied, *"Ah-ha, you don't! We're trying to nurture inconsistency, the kind of personalized response you'd get from a mom-and-pop shop."*

Managing inconsistency to achieve client service may sound very frightening, but think about where such "inconsistent" personalized response might be valuable to the overall goal of service to others. Think also of the difficulty of **"insuring** consistency" with as diverse a group as volunteers. You may find that through proper training, anticipating needs and sharing parameters, managed inconsistency becomes less formidable than trying to make every response exactly the same

It is a wise person that understands and accepts the fact that about the time we think we have all the answers, the questions change.

Keep It Simple

When thinking like an entrepreneur, there is a basic rule to keep in mind:

KEEP IT SIMPLE.

I had mentioned this in designing efforts through Leadershift, but it is so important that I believe it needs to be looked at again in discussing facets of entrepreneurial thinking.

As you design new pathways and actions to accomplish the mission of your program or projects within the program, I urge you to:

1. Keep processes, systems and work as simple as possible.

2. Involve those who will be doing the work, to gain their input on how best to do it.

3. Challenge everyone to find simpler ways to do the work; help them use technology as a tool for this.

4. Reward those that come up with these ideas.

5. Insure that everyone understands that the way it is first designed is not sacred.

6. Help people understand that changing things for the better, making them less complex and more direct, is encouraged and even commanded!

In embedding this philosophy in the minds of everyone who comes in contact with your department-volunteers, paid staff, clients, suppliers, organizational hierarchy and colleagues-you will hopefully unleash a new appreciation for simplification. (4-4)

You might even try some of these suggestions to get across how strongly you want to encourage simplicity:

1. Invent an example of a procedure for a specific job such as getting a mailing out; make it as ridiculously complex as possible. Share it and ask for better ways that could have been devised to accomplish the goal.

2. Then ask teams of people to review a real-life process that needs improvement and suggest simple ways to achieve its' objective.

3. Offer prizes to the team that does it the fastest; the team that is most creative; the team that designed their response in the least complicated group-process manner; the group that had the most fun, and the one which explained their answer in the simplest manner. (That should give you enough award categories to earn everyone a prize.)

4. Make it fun and extol the benefits of their answers, while pointing out that that is what you want from them on a continuing basis as you all search for ways to simplify efforts.

The result of establishing a norm of striving for simplification may extend to inspiring more creativity, seeing change as good, encouraging and constantly seeking improvement. All of these extensions would feed into the type of leadership needed to direct programs successfully in our changing world.

Thinking like an entrepreneur is a far cry from the traditional role of volunteer managers of old, who waited patiently in the wings until someone asked for help. These dedicated people thought of themselves as a servant and indeed they were. If the truth were to be told, we could probably find many entrepreneurs among their ranks, who found quiet but effective ways to bring creative thinking into their work.

In today's world, the role of volunteer program administrator is more pro-active, helping agencies and organizations thrive as volunteer and paid staff work as a team to accomplish goals. The role of servant has given way to a philosophy of servant-leader (4-5) for the program director, who understands the importance of power, the value of human and other resources, and proactively earns a role in the decision making circle of her organization.

Her greatest leverage is her own entrepreneurial stance that allows her to take risks, think innovatively and create new ways to achieve success, while serving the needs and interests of others. (4-6)

She's come a long way.

Innovation

List a new idea you have that might even be revolutionary:

List options for implementation. Rank them by which you feel might work best.

Consider the following (some will not apply to your circumstances):

...Who might oppose your #1 option above? Why?

...Are their objections valid? Why?

...How can you remove their objections?

...How might you win their support?

...What are the risk factors in implementing your idea?

...Who will be effected?

...What will the timing be?

...Who must be involved if the idea is to succeed?

...If this idea fails, what would the consequences be? Are these acceptable?

Empowerment

What do volunteers need to empower them? How can you provide this?

What information is necessary to empower volunteers? How can you provide this?

Think through specific job assignments... what things are NOT permissible for volunteers to do. (You empower people by giving them parameters so that they are protected from errors.)

Future Needs

Clients (or customers) have changing needs. To stay ahead of the need for responses, it is important to attempt to anticipate future needs. With key people, including volunteers, paid staff, specialists and clients themselves, brainstorm needs clients could have in the future and possible options for response that your volunteer department might offer.

As you discuss potential needs of clients, see if you can also identify some changes in the needs that volunteers or paid staff might have that would also impact services.

Simplifying

List the most complex thing that you have to do (or be involved with--a system, perhaps):

What is the goal of this process?

How could it be made simpler?

Does this simplified process still attain its original goal?

Who would you need to influence in order to change the process to this simpler form? How?

Characteristics of a Servant/Leader

Summarized from "The Servant as Leader" by Robert Greenleaf. Center for Applied Studies, Cambridge, MA

1. The servant/leader is servant first, to whom followers grant leadership after they have been well-served.

2. The servant/leader's openness to inspiration and insight provides vision and direction.

3. Invites others to go along and trusts them to do so.

4. Always knows and can articulate the bigger goal, the vision, the dream, which excites followers' imagination and sustains their spirits.

5. Is an intent listener, knowing that genuine listening both builds strength in others and provides information for problem solving.

6. Can take the abstract idea and facilitate the hearer's "leap of imagination" drawn from the hearer's own personal experience so it all makes sense.

7. Can systematically neglect the less important while choosing to do the more important.

8. Knows when to withdraw and regroup or take time for reorientation.

9. Accepts person unqualifiedly; never rejects person, but may reject performance.

10. Empathizes with others by being able to get into their shoes. Genuine interest in and affection for the followers.

11. Can tolerate imperfection in self and others.

12. Uses own intuitive insight to bridge the gap in available information to make decisions, and has good record of right decisions. Knows when to decide.

13. Possesses foresight about what is going to happen when in the future, and the ethical resolve to act on that while action is still possible.

14. Thorough preparation for a situation, with faith that if one releases the analytical thought processes, a solution will appear from the creative deeps.

15. Ability to be on two levels of consciousness always: 1) in the real world, involved and responsible; and 2) detached and standing outside the real world, seeing it in the long sweep of history and future.

16. Is aware of life and the environment in a way that gives own intuitive computers a lot of data to work with.

17. Believes that in the stress of real life one can compose oneself in a way that permits the creative process to provide answers. An inner serenity.

18. Persuasion, rather than coercion, convinces one to change.

19. Knows who he or she is able to be, own person, choosing own role.

20. Perserverance: one step at a time toward the goal in spite of frustrations.

21. Can conceptualize change and instill the spirit to work for change in those who have to accomplish the change.

22. Can wait until the group of people can define their own need for wholeness or healing.

23. The servant/leader is motivated for work by own need for wholeness or healing.

24. Believes that only in community is an individual healed and made whole.

25. Views institutions as necessary to our survival, but believes they must become people-building institutions, not people-destroying institutions.

26. Understands that those leaders who stand outside the institution but who are charged with seeing that the institutions is making progress toward its goals are the very leaders who have the greatest potential for raising the quality of the whole society. They need to be servant/leaders.

27. Recognizes coercive power because he/she has been exposed to it and knows its bitterness. He or she could use it but chooses not to because it diminishes the followers.

28. Knows that change must start inside oneself, not "out there"; that all problems are inside oneself, not "out there."

29. Recognizes "the enemy" as strong natural servants who have the potential to lead, but do not lead, or who choose to follow a nonservant.

30. Recognizes that preparation to lead must become a top priority.

Serving Needs of Others

Entrepreneurial thinking demands an understanding of specific needs for which the entrepreneur can devise responses. The volunteer administrator is constantly alert for needs (expressed or unexpressed) throughout the organization that could be met by appropriate volunteer placement.

....

NEEDS of (Person or Dept.)	For (work assignment)	Could be filled by (Vol. w/skills of....)

....

....

Best way to get key people to accept and own the volunteer involvement:

Chapter Five

Inspiring Creativity

I was an avid comic book reader when I was a child, and always loved to see the light bulb drawn over the head of a character because I knew that the story was going to take a wonderful and brilliant turn! This simple symbol announced to readers that a great idea had come into his or her head and they were about to turn even the most desperate situation in a new direction.

If I were being asked to draw a cartoon of what a typical volunteer leader must look like to thrive into our new century, I would put that same light bulb over her head to symbolize the need for continual, creative thinking. I assume that such thinking has been part of the skills volunteer administrators have had in the past, but believe strongly that our current times demand a much higher level of competency in this area.

That sounds easier than it is.

For creativity to become a guiding force in any size or style program, an incredible array of demands is added to any leader's shoulders as they must:

........Set up an environment where creative thinking can thrive.
........Inspire creativity among workers through stimulation & recognition.
........Model creative thinking in their work.
........Keep everyone focused on the mission while encouraging creative "tangents".
........Stay personally creative.
........Evaluate creative ideas for those that will be most effective.
........Have the strength of character to set great ideas aside because they do not
           contribute to the mission or fit the moment.

If that brings to mind the image of a juggler, you've gotten the picture!

The Creative Environment

In the last chapter of this book, I'll go into greater examination of the climate or setting in which work is done. Here however, let's look at the specific aspects of the environment or "feel" of the workplace that must exist for creative thinking to emerge and grow.

The environment of a truly creative workplace is rather easy to spot when you visit it, yet difficult to explain when describing it to others or trying to replicate it. Most of us end up with some vague statement such as, "well, I can't really explain it, but it just FELT alive and creative."

As non-specific as that statement seems, it actually has touched on the essence of any environment we try to describe to others.....it is the FEEL of a setting. Think back to times when you have had to go to an office, a company, a meeting or even a social event and felt that somehow you had entered hostile territory. If someone later asks you to define exactly what happened that gave you that feeling, you would probably find it difficult to site specific occurrences.

I would trust that in the environment that seemed less than friendly, no one actually was openly rude, threw hot coffee in your face or kicked you in the shins (definite signs of hostility!), but more subtle clues told the hair on the back of your neck to stand at watchful attention for predators.

Our youngest son Bob calls on large printing firms that have bought software from his employer, the Graphic Imaging Division of DuPont Corporation. After just a few weeks on the job, he shared that the "feelings" in client's offices were so palatable that he could almost predict within the first hour of his visit just how easy or tough it was going to be to train workers there in the use of his company's new software.

What Bob was sensing was the environment in a workplace, recognizing the incredible effect that has on the people there and their productivity and effectiveness.

For a volunteer program administrator to create and support an environment in which creative thinking can thrive, specific things must be in place before you witness light bulbs going off over people's heads.

The Understanding of Norms

Norms are simply the unwritten rules that govern behavior. They produce the environment in which rules of behavior set the standards for how people act and react.

The truly effective leader of volunteer programs will be very sensitive to norms that are already established, which additional ones need to be introduced to encourage creativity, and which others, that inhibit such freedom, need to be purged. Such understanding and finesse will take you to a new level of competency.

To accomplish this, you will first have to examine the norms or unwritten rules that already exist and identify those that are non-negotiable (typically mandated by authorities). Hold a brain-storming session with workers to identify the rules that they sense and that tell them how to behave. If it is difficult to stimulate honest sharing of such rules, you may wish to suggest categories in which norms might exist and offer specific examples you have noted. See the worksheets at the end of this chapter to help you with this.

Norms typically exist in categories such as organizational demands, recognition, punctuality, ethics and standards, support, supervision, attention to details, after-hour relationships, comfort and conflict. (5-1) Please be aware also, that the degree of difficulty you experience in getting your workers to share their thoughts openly is a clue to the climate around you....the more reluctance you encounter the more "closed" or "up-tight" your environment is; the more easily workers share their thoughts, the more open and creative it probably is! This exercise can be your first diagnostic test of the feel of your work setting.

It is critical for you as the leader to uncover the unwritten rules that govern behavior and then work to eradicate those that have a negative influence while encouraging or establishing those that are positive. Be careful with those that may be less than positive but are imposed by administration. When such negatives are identified, use creative thinking on ways they might be changed and ways to live with them in the meantime.

As you consider your norms, pay particular attention to those that impact creativity, such as:

☞ *Is it o.k. for people to come up with and share new ideas?. . . . .*

Or as soon as someone does, are they met with the idea-killers who shout, "We've never done it THAT way! We've always done it THIS way!" ..... or those awful, prejudicial responses of: "You're too young/new to the program, dearie, to understand."

☞ *Do people feel free to throw out any idea that pops into their heads as an issue is being discussed?. . .*

Or when they do, does everyone in the group glare or laugh at them to send a message of "what a stupid idea!" before the group goes on, ignoring the suggestion and its possible validity?

☞ *When a problem arises, what is everyone's first response?....*

Do they feel that they must go to the rule book to look up answers in order to "follow the company line", or go to a higher authority to ask what to do? Are they fearful of trying to devise their own solution?

☞ *When workers get ideas where must they take them?....*

Is there a strict procedure and chain of command that must be adhered to or can they bring it up in a meeting where everyone is hearing it for the first time?

☞ *Is it o.k. for anyone to question rulings, procedures, systems and dictates?.....*

Or are they met with reprimands, accusations of "Not being a good team-player" or branded a "trouble-maker"?

All of the above questions relate to the environment or climate factors that influence creativity. If norms exist in your organization which discourage creative thinking, it is important for you to identify them and find ways to get rid of them. Conversely, when you find norms that encourage and stimulate creative thinking, you will want to strengthen and preserve them.

The simple act of having co-workers examine the unwritten rules that govern the behavior in your programs will send a positive message to everyone working there:

We want to do all we can to encourage creative thinking and remove any barriers that might prevent anyone from being as creative as possible!

It's a good message and tends to produce light bulbs over the heads of a lot of folks.

Characteristics of a Creative Environment

I have tried to point out examples that are negative in the section above, but let me tell you that rarely, as I consult with groups, do I find all negatives. For the most part I find some are good and some are not as good. I then work with leaders to sort norms into either category, deciding what behavior they want to encourage to help them focus on their mission. You might also do this same exercise, understanding that every program's list will be unique, as it is personalized to the demands and needs of the agency, clientele, demographics, etc.

A response to a crisis will be different for workers in a hospice setting, for example, than for someone who works in a library. In the hospice, rules that govern blood-borne pathogens (AIDS or Hepatitis B) MUST be followed; in the library the worker would have more room to create her own response to an emergency. This would mean that rules that govern behavior of a hospice volunteer in times of crisis would necessarily be different than those that govern the library volunteer.

Take a look at the following list I have used in working with groups, that might encourage a positive environment for creativity. Think creatively in adjusting this list to your own setting.

A group that wishes to stimulate creativity among its members:

1. Includes all perspectives in discussion, not just those that agree with how things are being done at the present. Keep in mind the following considerations:

    a. Paid staff, volunteers, clients, client-families, suppliers, parallel workers and experts/advisors can offer different view points regarding the same effort and assist in effectively planning actions that take these into consideration.

    b. Gathering only "yes-people" around you does not stimulate creative thinking in anyone, including yourself. Dictators throughout the centuries have made this mistake, beheading those who offered a different response to a question and dared to disagree with the leader. Too late, such dictators typically recognize that rather than beheading them, they should have listened and understood what was being said.

    c. The person who cares about the success of the effort and plays the Devil's Advocate role can be invaluable to a secure, open-minded leader. For any effort to work, especially if it is a highly creative and innovative one, leaders must look at the down-side, envision any problems the action may create and then determine if the problems are acceptable.

    d. Avoid the "Ehore"* syndrome person who is always negative simply for the sake of the attention it will gain. This person is usually just trying to be obnoxious, as opposed to the true devil's advocate who is trying to play a positive role.

    *The always gloom-predicting donkey from Winnie-the-Pooh fame.

I will offer one word of caution about this last point: keep in mind that even a paranoid person is occasionally right, and your Ehore may actually be correct in his/her less-than-positive response to a new idea, so always look objectively at the argument. To distinguish an Ehore from those who can play the role of Devil's Advocate, note that Ehore wallows and even delights in the negativity; her counter-part moves on to problem-solving and turning lemons into lemonade. A big difference.

2. Allows anyone to question anything; no "sacred cows" exist. (5-2)

    a. With only the constraints of no personal attacks, blaming, or breach of confidences, creative groups allow and even encourage members to question everything: policies, systems, procedures, "but-we-always activities", lines of authority, services or products, goals, traditions, assumptions, etc. etc.

        The goal is always the same: come up with a better idea; find a simpler path; define it more clearly; make it better. The goal is never to wallow in negatives, but to move on, learning from any bad or non-productive experiences. Nothing is labeled a failure, because every experience has a lesson in it; learning that lesson turns every negative into a potential for positive action.

    b. Too many groups hold on to out-dated systems or procedures because the person who introduced it is so revered. Help folks to understand that moving away from a traditional response does not negate the contribution or value of either the older action OR the person who created it. Don't confuse worth and work; you do not label an older effort as "worthless" when you set it aside, you simply see it as a building block of the past that enabled today's successes......and it does not in any way diminish the respect for the contributor who first brought it into existence.

        Such thinking stifles creativity dramatically and causes workers to have to detour around efforts, systems and procedures that are obstructions of success.

    c. One of the best ways to demonstrate your commitment to the "no sacred cows" norm, is to invite people you evaluate to evaluate *your* supervision of them. Some of the most valuable feedback I got from those I supervised at Project Concern International, was the last question on their evaluation form: "How might I have supported you more effectively?" Such a question invites positive suggestions that can stimulate greater effectiveness and says to everyone, "It's o.k. to risk saying what you think and to express your needs."

    d. Encourage people to "go outside the lines" when thinking of new ways to accomplish goals. If parameters exist such as the example I gave you regarding Hospice volunteers who might come in contact with a patient's blood, tell folks about the parameters and why they must be honored. Do so in simple terms and in a straight-forward manner to insure understanding and to model "non-negotiation".

3. Groups that wish to stimulate creativity never allow personal attacks or blaming for things that have gone wrong. They identify problems by the trouble they have caused, the lives that were effected and their root cause. They are not interested in placing blame on people, but do want to know the source of the problem so they can prevent it from happening again.

> Example: The productive program does not focus on how badly Jammie Johnson goofed when offering a diabetic patient a candy bar, but on how workers can understand the consequences of giving inappropriate snacks to patients, determine what might be appropriate and how to respond when patients beg for inappropriate favors.

4. Groups wanting to stimulate creativity do not try to over-regulate actions.

Sometimes, in response to problems, groups will over-react and attempt to control behavior unrealistically; others may be led by people who need such rigid control that they cannot allow suggestions that would deviate from what has already been prescribed.

In both cases the result is the same: a stifling of creativity. If, for any reason, extraordinary control is demanded, there is little room for new thinking, different approaches or innovation.

Groups that exhibit such rigidity rarely attract and almost never retain creative thinkers. Such behavior clearly sends the message that change and creative thinking is unwanted.

The older the group, the more likely you are to find over-regulation. A healthy group constantly monitors its rules, norms and guiding principles to insure that they are free from such creativity-killers.

Keep in mind that over-regulation is typically a result of people who need control. Not everyone can do well in a group that invites collective, integrated, creative thinking. If you encounter someone who simply can't adjust to such non-controlling norms, it might be kind of you to let them find some other setting where they can control their surroundings and change is not likely to occur. (5-3)

Removing Obstacles to Creativity

In both the discussion of re-shaping programs and creating an environment in which creativity can thrive, we have been looking at different facets of the same concept:

> *Our goal is not to force people into saying "yes" to creativity,*
> *but rather to remove obstacles to them saying "no" to it.*

Look around you; examine your surroundings, meetings, procedures, norms, demands, relationships; study the way your group communicates, its attitudes and actions in relation to team-building, growth, pleasure, energy use, expectations, etc.

Among that field of characteristics and actions are there things that inhibit creativity? Let me share a true story that is a classic example of stifling creativity:

A new employee came to work in a Louisiana textile mill in the late 1960's. He noted that one machine, hated by all workers, was jamming constantly, causing the assembly line to be stopped, workers to stand idle and snags to appear in the textile being processed.

Eager to make a good impression, he watched the machine carefully, found that in one stage of the process one action was causing a roller to be jammed, thus creating the long, negative chain of events. After his shift one night he took exact measurements of the critical parts of the machine and drew up sketches to show how the problem could be rectified.

Excitedly he took the plans to the plant manager and began, "I've figured out what the problem is on the machine....." but was interrupted by the manager who admonished him by saying, "You've only been here a few weeks. That problem has been looked at by a dozen men far more experienced and educated than you, and none of them could fix it, so I don't think somebody like you could do so. Just do your job and keep your ideas to yourself; I don't have time for foolishness."

So the employee went back to his work, did his job and kept all of his ideas to himself. Later, when a new manager came on the scene, he saw the problems the machine caused and called all the workers together, asking who might know what the problem was and how to fix it.

Apparently schooled in body language, the new manager spotted our innovative worker who had remained silent while everyone else voiced their frustration about the problems the machine caused. The manager then asked the worker directly if he had noted the problems.

"Yes sir," the worker replied.

"Do you know how to fix it?" asked the manager.

"Yes sir," the worker said.

At this point the manager asked the worker to demonstrate his thinking, and when he did, the manager and several of the workers immediately saw the real problem and that the worker's suggestion to fix it was both simple and workable.

After the others had left, the manager turned to the worker and said, "Why didn't you say anything before?"

"I did sir, when I first began to work here, but the old manager told me to mind my own business 'cause I was too new and young to know how to fix the machine. He told me to shut up and do my job. And that's what I've done. I was just waiting for somebody to come along and ask me how to fix it, and then I'd tell them. You came, you asked and now I've told you, but it sure would have been easier on all of us if it hadn't taken 15 years!"

Fifteen years of frustration, worn equipment, lost revenue and wasted time; 15 years of a creative mind behind a sealed mouth. I've often wondered how many other great ideas the worker had but never shared; I would guess a lot.

The worker was stifled by a boss who assumed a new employee could not possibly have come up with a better idea to solve a problem. In this example it was the boss himself who was the obstacle, not only to creative thinking, but to welcoming that thinking out in the open for careful review and experimentation.

When looking at identifying and removing any obstacles to creative thinking and expression, take a long, hard look first at yourself and then at others that might be holding people's ideas back because of their attitude, messages or demeanor. If those people in authority or at a peer level convey any of the following messages, either consciously or unconsciously to workers, you can bet your bottom dollar creative thinking will vanish in thin air:

> ....You? An original idea? I doubt it!
> ....You're too new to understand.
> ....I don't recall you having experience in that.
> ....That's not your job, so forget it!
> ....You're over your head; cool it.
> ....We're the experts here!
> ....Your last idea was a bomb; why should I listen to a new one?
> ....We've found the old ways best.
> ....Write that up; I'll read it when I have some free time.
> ....Might have some merit; go through channels and we'll see who likes it.
> ....Did you clear this with Mr. XYZ?
> ....You haven't finished your own assignment; why are you spending time on this?
> ....It's not a good time for me right now; wait till I get back to you later.
> ....We've got enough to do already; why are you bothering me with something new?
> ....Stop drinking caffeinated coffee! It makes you come up with stuff I can't handle!
> ....Your kind of people don't usually come up with good ideas, but I suppose I could
>   look at it sometime. Not now though. I'll call you.

In an honest assessment, you will also have to look at more subtle messages that really convey mistrust, jealousy, prejudice, assumptions or in rare cases, simple meanness. (5-4)

Watch especially for reactions and sabotage to new ideas from those who really plan to take credit for the idea later. Watch also for procedures that are so Byzantine and complex that innovators decide it's not worth the hassle to try to submit them in "proper form" to higher authorities.

Walt Disney is known for his artistry on film and the drawing board, but also because of his gift of inspiring creativity. His engineers who designed and built Disneyland were and are called "Imagineers". Subtle message, great results! He also believed in MBWA.... "Management by Walking Around", because he said he could pick up so many more creative ideas.

Several management gurus have made a fortune since Walt in promoting this as a new management practice and even have day-long seminars on it. I can't imagine spending a whole day trying to explain to anyone with an IQ over 75 that the best way to encourage others is to walk around and get to know them and what they are doing. It seems so obvious and opens the lines of communication between bosses and workers .

> "Hi Jim, I'm Walt. What'cha doing? Looks good. Any ideas on how to make it
> easier? Anything I can do to help? Had any great light bulbs pop on over you as
> you thought of a great idea for us? Yeah?....well tell me, I'm all ears!"

Not a tough concept to grasp. When people care about others and what they are thinking about; when they talk to them like the colleague they are rather than through layers of managerial flim-flam and "channels"; when they respect their intelligence and are not threatened by how good they are, neat things happen.

And it doesn't take 15 years.

Watch for barriers to creative thinking; roadblocks to people connecting across titles, levels and management-chart boxes. It's Leadershift in action, and when it's in place, you'll probably have to put on sunglasses because of all the light bulbs going off!

Rewarding Creativity

There is a simple rule of thumb in organizational and human behavior:

You get more of what you reward; less of what you ignore or punish.

One great way to establish an environment for creativity, is to have innovative ways to recognize workers who have come up with new ideas.

I do not mean that you only plan a wing-ding of an annual recognition banquet, but that you find unique ways throughout the year to reward creative thinking.

Recognition is not any single event, no matter how wonderful, but a series of creative ways to reward, recognize and acclaim the good works of volunteers and staff. All of these efforts together produce an on-going process that is critical to success. For such a process to be in place, it requires what I call an "appreciation-commitment."

For an agency or program to have an "appreciation-commitment", the people at the very top of the leadership must see recognition as an integral part of working with people. This translates into a constant effort to appreciate and respect people beyond any confines of what we normally define as "recognition".

When there is a commitment to expressing appreciation, it is extended to everyone who comes in contact with you. When that appreciation embraces those people who come up with creative thinking, you are telling the world how much you value creativity, and by so doing, typically attract new innovative thinkers.

There may be no more valuable tool in your effort to inspire creativity than that of sincere, open recognition for those who offer light-bulb thinking.

There may also be no greater challenge than to devise clever and fun ways to say thank you to such people either! I urge you to involve everyone in designing personalized and innovative ways to appreciate others. (5-5)

Enabling creativity by establishing an environment where it can flourish, removing obstacles to innovative thinking and finding ways to recognize such contributions is a major challenge for every leader.

For volunteer program leaders to be truly effective in their work, they will have to rise to totally new levels of competency in this area.

Creatively!

The Creative Environment

Norms, those unwritten rules that govern behavior, must help people be creative. Consider which norms now exist in your organization that support creativity and therefore encourage new ideas and approaches. Typically they are found in the following categories:

Organizational Demands:

Recognition:

Conflict:

Support:

Supervision:

Relationships:

Physical Surroundings:

Communication:

If, in the process of identifying positive norms, you uncover negative ones, how will you remove them?

If you can think of other norms that could further creativity, how might you introduce and sustain them?

Barriers to Creativity

Truly creative groups allow and even encourage people to question anything...policies, systems, procedures, activities, authority, assumptions, etc. When constraints are imposed, telling people for example, that they cannot question systems, creativity declines.

Are there issues or areas that volunteers or paid staff cannot question? Are they legitimate constraints such as immunizations in health care facilities or are they personal control issues that simply discourage new ideas?

How might you remove, reduce or realistically find a way to live with imposed barriers to creativity?

Over-Regulation

Review the systems and processes that govern work in your organization. Are there those that attempt to over-control efforts? Are there those that have become so complex through the years that they desperately need simplification?

Look at each identified issue. How can you relax or simplify each?

If you recognize that changing ultra-complex or stringent rules or processes is beyond your control, how can you find ways to live with this reality and reduce the stress they cause?

Getting Rid of "Put-Downs"

In a brainstorming session with volunteers and/or paid staff, discuss how hurtful negative comments or "put-downs" are and how they inhibit creativity and innovative problem-solving. Being careful to establish a ground rule of NOT pointing fingers at any personalities, ask people to list "put-downs" they have received or heard. Discuss why each was negative and what such statements might feel like:

Conclude by having people discuss the best ways to eliminate any subtle or overt "put-downs" from interactions and ways to respond positively should one come their way. Discuss the difference in how people interpret messages from others; often people can take a statement as a "put-down" that was never intended to be one. How can people distinguish between direct feedback and "put-downs"?

Rewarding Creativity

What creative ideas can you think of to reward people for innovative ideas or solutions to problems?

Chapter Six

Creative Recognition

In looking at the changing roles of volunteer program administrators and the new competencies they must demonstrate, I believe that we cannot overlook that of creative recognition.

Recognition of volunteers has grown from overseeing banquets, pins and plaques to instilling and standing guard over an agency-wide commitment to appreciation that extends beyond the walls of any program and is aimed UP & OUTWARD as well as DOWN & INWARD through management ranks. At its most basic, our task is to devise new, creative and clever ways to sincerely thank anyone who helps us and to do so in a meaningful way.

The best way to find creative ways to say thank you to people is to ask their peers to make suggestions. Hold a brainstorm session and ask for fun, creative and poignant ways to reward folks for their contributions. Ask them to widen their thinking to simple ways to show more respect; because 99% of programs today are culturally diverse, be sure you ask people within that diversity what might be appropriate and meaningful. (6-1)

Keep in mind that recognition is user-oriented. For a recognition effort to truly be appreciated by individuals and/or groups, it must be meaningful to them. The reclusive donor who gets her picture on the front page of the local newspaper won't feel very good because it goes against her need for privacy.

The gregarious volunteer who loves crowds of people and parties, won't writhe in glee if you send him a certificate through the mail, and a supplier who donated two weeks of labor to remodel your office may be less than happy with only a pat on the back at the end of the effort!

In two of my books, *Secrets of Motivation* and *Beyond, Banquets, Plaques & Pins*, I go into detail on the importance of understanding the people or groups (yes, groups have personalities, motivations and needs just as individuals do) you are trying to recognize. In those works I relied heavily on David McClelland's motivational categories which help us distinguish primary motivations of achievement, power and affiliation, so that rewards are in line with these categories.

In both books I also offered hundreds of ideas that might fill the needs of dozens of "categories" of folks beyond these three personality types. Categories include youth, senior, working women, men, lower income, etc. and in settings such as churches, youth groups, hospital, health care, schools, etc.

Your list of categories will be unique to your own setting, but let me share some of the ideas I've used through the years in some categories you may not have thought of. I do this because I believe the list broadens the thinking about who needs to be recognized and appreciated as we expand our definition of recognition

Agent Publics: Those people or groups who speak on your behalf; referral agents not on your payroll, but who frequently send supporters, volunteers, clients, and others in your direction when they deem it appropriate. For example, the ministers, school official, police or health personnel who refer people to crisis programs. These are _agent publics_ and are critical to success of the agency. (6-2)

Creative ways to recognize:

> ....Write a feature story on how they steered folks in your direction and what great things happened in the lives of those people because of this. Focus on those served and the servers themselves.

> ....Send a plaque that they can display in their offices.

> ....If they have a newsletter, openly thank them in it for their service.

> ....Invite a small group of key people from their group to attend your annual banquet. Recognize them openly at that time; give something tangible they can take back to their place of business.

> ....Find out how they get reward within their own profession, i.e.: Media = FCC; schools = National Education Ass'n; health care = their accrediting body or professional association, etc. etc. Write to that entity and tell them about the good the local group has done for you; find out if that entity has a newsletter.... if so, write a feature story for the publication to honor their help.

> ....Find ways to recognize individuals within their own organization, with such things as letters to their supervisor, CEO etc.

> ....Include key agents in planning sessions; if they are part of your intake route for clients, supporters etc. they will offer a very valuable perspective and may be able to help you become even more effective; including their vantage point will help you and project the message that you respect and value them.

Suppliers: Those individuals or groups which supply the things you need to do your work. Typically there are stores or companies which provide you with your needs on an on-going basis: the variety store that offers you a discount on gifts and items you buy throughout the year; the office supply company that makes sure your order gets to you quickly when you run out of even your most unique need; the jeweler who engraves your plaques and trophies and can always come up with 14 more pins than you ordered at the last minute, and the company that sells you the uniforms you need each year.

***Be very careful not to cross any lines of propriety you or your organization have established in thanking suppliers. Only you can determine what is appropriate. Avoid any effort that might be misinterpreted or create an obligation; you will want to be free to change suppliers as needs change.*

Creative Ways to Recognize:

.... If the person that you deal with is an employee, write a thank you letter that details their extra effort and helpful ways and send it to their employer or boss, asking that it be placed in their personnel file. Send a copy to the person so they know it is part of their record of work.

.... Tell the supplier that you will be happy to offer recommendations to other potential buyers or clients on their good service.

.... Invite them to your recognition gala; present a tangible gift they can display or wear at their place of business.

.... Write a feature story and take a picture of the supplier with a client or leader from your program; put it in the local papers and send a copy to any publication in the supplier's field (i.e.: plumber = national association of plumbers).

.... If you have some form of "membership" (auxiliary, volunteer corps, etc.), make them an honorary member at one of your events; take a picture for local media.

....When setting up a focus group to examine a new project idea, include them and their perspective; respecting someone's viewpoint and asking for their input says, "We appreciate you and need your insight to help us do a better job."

.... Find out if they belong to a chamber of commerce in your area; if so, go to a meeting and recognize them in front of their peers; get media coverage.

Supporters: This category is very broad and can include donors, volunteer experts, door-openers, advisors, those who steer you through complex procedures, those who defend you in difficult times, ... volunteers in all kinds of hats!

Creative Ways to Recognize:

....Discover as much as you can about the individuals..... hobbies, collections, pets, favorite locations, family profile, home towns, schools attended, club and church affiliations, favorite colors, sports, etc. Tailor gifts and recognitions to these: the collector of chess pieces gets a book on famous collections or something to add to their own; the person who loves to fish is given a new rod, fishing vest or book on "All The Ones That Got Away!"; the music lover gets a favorite performers latest CD, etc.

....For the person at who is at your site frequently, "name" the coffee pot after them for a month; put a silly sign on it with something like, "Just like Jan Jones, this coffee pot is here to serve you." Use humor appropriately but cleverly when possible.

....Write a letter to family members expressing "Thanks for sharing (name/relationship) with us, she really helped our clients by leading XXXX event and we know that your support of her was a big factor in her being able to give us so much time. We appreciate your support of our work through your support at home for her." or, to parents of a young volunteer, "(Name) has done such a wonderful job helping us this past month that I wanted to take a minute to say thank you for raising such a great young person. He's making a difference here because you instilled in him the value of helping others; thanks for your continued support of him as he works with our clients."

....Write to donors of goods, services or dollars and share specifically what their contribution meant in terms of people helped; tell a particular story that links their donation to the betterment of life of those your program serves.

....Send a holiday card to supporters from a client helped; personalize it.

....If you have supporters for a program which you might not think of as "clients", such as people who attend arts and cultural events, re-shape your thinking to see them as a consumer (another name for client) as well as your supporters.

Keep lists of such folks and send a holiday card (New Years cards offer especially creative opportunities) with an up-beat message: "Hi. My name is Tommy Tuba. I may not be the most popular instrument in the Billings Symphony Orchestra, but I've got the biggest heart and I hope to see you sometime soon. I'll watch for you at one of our Spring concerts and you'll know I'm saying a special hello just for you when I nod in your direction and give out a great big "OOMPA!" .... Silly? Of course, but it will get the reader's attention and remind them of the good times they have had at past performances. Obviously, an orchestra schedule would be included with the card and at some time in the performances, the tuba player needs to nod his instrument and give out with a particularly poignant "OOMPA!" This can start an 'inside-joke' that can do more good than a dozen ad campaigns, by the way.

Media: No matter what your agency or program offers in the way of public and human services, the media will be a part of your life. Recognizing those good journalists, television and radio people and others involved with media outlets in your area is not only good business, it is smart business.

Many times clients, client-loved ones, supporters, donors and volunteers find their way to your doorstep because of something written or spoken about by media personnel. To insure that this avenue to your door is enlightened, current and friendly, it is wise to identify those people within the media ranks who have made outstanding contributions to your efforts and recognize them creatively. (6-3)

Creative Ways to Recognize:

....Find ways to honor them in front of their peers; TV stations compete for local emmys; newspaper writers for national and local awards. Can you find a way to honor them at ceremonies giving these accolades?

....Make individuals part of your group identity: give T-shirts with your program name and emblem to TV and radio personalities; "membership" plaques to reporters, etc.

....If they will play a major role in bringing the spotlight to an event, consider re-naming the event to include their name, i.e. the Indianapolis Walk for Mankind, brought to you by Project Concern International and WTTX, Channel 11's top television station.

Recognition of individuals and groups can offer an exciting opportunity for creative thinking as you work to recognize and appreciate their contributions to the people you serve. By involving many others in coming up with innovative and fun ways to say "thank you", you will further the commitment to appreciation of everyone who touches your work and deserves heart-felt gratitude.

As you design your recognition initiatives, keep these factors in mind:

1. Recognition is user-oriented.

2. The more you know about a person/group, the more you can personalize reward.

3. Recognition is more intangible than tangible; it is best built on a relationship of respect and appreciation that is transmitted in everyday language and action.

4. If you want new ideas on how to recognize someone, ask their acquaintances.

5. Find opportunities to recognize good works externally; find settings important to the contributor and reward them openly there.

6. Personal notes of thanks hand-written (or with hand-written postscripts) by someone in authority are most meaningful.

7. Tap into the wide world of organizational publications to find new sites to display your appreciation for folks or groups.

8. Never give recognition because of what it will do for you; give it because you sincerely want to honor others.

9. Never give recognition when it is not deserved; everyone around will lose respect for the giver and the receiver will usually feel belittled.

10. Vary recognition efforts; make sure you are not tailoring rewards to what YOU would like.

11. Have fun with ideas for recognition; encourage people to "play" with ideas but make sure the "play" is never harmful. Roasts are wonderful if handled carefully, but can offer horror stories if inappropriate.

12. Give recognition unexpectedly; a candy kiss and quick note of thanks on a staff person's desk on February 22nd can warm the heart because it is a surprise.

13. Keep good records of recognitions, so that you can vary rewards to those who are around a long time.

14. Simple respect on a day to day basis and warm, specific thank yous are still the best tools for building a good recognition process.

Recognition is all about relationships. It is a tangible way to appreciate the contributions of others and reinforce the importance of working with together.

For the modern leader of any volunteer program, it is much, much more than the traditionally narrower confines of plaques, pins and banquets for volunteers. Instead it is an on-going process that reaches out to everyone with whom you interact and says, "We value you and how you help us."

It is targeted, personal and appropriate. It is frequent, sincere and specific, and it happens throughout the year in ways that make the volunteers and paid staff know that their contributions are recognized and appreciated.

It is playful and poignant, creative and careful, measured and meaningful...Here are a few ideas that can be used with either paid or volunteer staff members:

☞ Name the refrigerator in the staff lounge after a person "filled with good cheer"...

☞ Write a letter to the family of a worker to say "thank you for sharing your loved one with us; we appreciate your support as he/she does xxxxxxxx."

☞ Have reserved parking spaces for the volunteer or paid staff people of the month.

☞ Have buttons that say "We love staff" printed and worn by volunteers; have staff wear buttons that say, "We love volunteers."

☞ Declare a paid staff appreciation day or week; celebrate it much like volunteer week.

☞ Recognize full teams of paid and volunteer staff; honor their accomplishments in the agency newsletter.

☞ Make sure that you provide as many "comforts" as possible in your work environment such as coat racks, secure areas for purses, designated parking spaces, a place to relax, coffee & snacks, enough space to do assigned work (desk, table, etc.), proper air temperatures, good lighting, convenient supplies, access to washrooms, a central point for information such as a bulletin board, comfortable work furniture, personalized work space, etc. All of these things and many more in the physical surroundings tell workers you care about them; they also are a great motivator when present and a **de-**motivator if neglected.

☞ Send stories about the good individuals are doing to their community newspaper, their hometown newspaper (often a different location), alumnae magazine, professional journal, church or community organization newsletter, etc. Find periodicals that are part of the person's life outside of your site, and praise your worker to his or her peers there.

☞ Leave mysterious notes of appreciation in worker's mailboxes, simply signed "your secret admirer's."

☞ Send inexpensive children's valentines to workers at times other than Feb. 14th.

☞ Keep a file of birthdays, anniversaries and special dates and send a note or card.

☞ Ask administration and board leaders to send letters or notes of appreciation to workers; give them a specific effort to mention in their correspondence. Copy these notes to their personnel files.

☞ If you can find someone who can do good cartoons of people, have them create appropriate drawings that highlight a person's contributions and place them around your site. Gather and frame them after they have been on display for a time, and permanently hang them in a common eating area in the same manner famous restaurants hang drawings or photos of celebrities who have eaten there.

☞ Create a "walk (or wall) of fame" at your site; honor workers by having their name added to a brick or tile (a local high school art teacher can tell you how to do this) for a permanent recognition. Make sure this honor is among your highest and therefore not given lightly!

☞ Name several awards after outstanding volunteers or paid staff and give this honor annually or monthly; submit a story to media each time they are given, telling of the contributions of the new honoree and the person for whom the award is named.

☞ If your agency is inter-connected to a computer system, have a message of congratulations for outstanding work flash on the screen when it is opened; put the recognition message on eveyone's E-mail too.

☞ Sponsor decorating contests of work space at holidays; give silly prizes to everyone.

☞ Have a Kids work with Mom/Dad/Grandparent etc. days when children are invited to come and see where their relative works, what they do and who they work with.

☞ If you have a CEO that is willing, hold a contest for people to "Be the Boss for a Day" and work along-side your top administrator... you may be amazed at what teamwork follows as a staff person comes to appreciate all that is on the CEO's shoulders!

☞ When trainings are being held for paid staff on issues that impact anyone....wellness, communication, new trends, etc...... offer attendance to volunteers; try to empower as many ways as possible that volunteers and paid staff share learning experiences together; it will honor volunteers, send subtle messages to paid workers and foster team building.

☞ Personalize coffee mugs.

☞ Hold "Heritage Days" potlucks where everyone who wishes to do so, brings a food treat typical to their nationality. Mark each with the name of the contributor and country represented and have it available at the staff's central meeting point so everyone can enjoy the diversity of tastes! If someone says, "I don't know what heritage to use.", challenge them to bring a dish from a pretend-country. (That would come in handy for me, as I'm German-Irish-English-Scottish. I'd probably bring something native to Door County, Wisconsin and call it "Cherries Jubilee from Doorca-Cheeseia" just for the fun of it!)

The list can go on and on. The two books I mentioned previously in this chapter hold over 500 such "light bulbs!", but you get the picture here.

Recognition is a continuing challenge and may be the most serious business you will be about as you insure that everyone who works with your program is honored, respected and continually valued in ways that are meaningful to them.

It is most certainly, a competency that every effective volunteer program leader must have and continually update through the years.

Creative Recognition

It's good to do an assessment of the forms of recognition given to volunteers and paid staff on a regular basis. Doing so may help to spark new ideas and evaluate the appropriateness of current efforts.

Recognition is an on-going process that is dynamic, changing as people and times change. It may be beneficial to involve several perspectives in the assessment of recognition for your program or organization.

Tangible Recognition (pins, banquets, etc.)

Do Now	Have done in past; could still do	New Ideas

Intangible Recognition (praise, fun, social opportunities, etc.)

Do Now	Have done in past, could still do	New Ideas

Agent Publics

List people who work on the fringes of your program, but who are important to your work because they speak on your behalf, refer clients or volunteers, vouch for your program's veracity, help convince potential funders or supporters to give you resources, etc.

Create a card file for these people or computerize your information for ready retrieval & updates.

Media

List contacts and information on media in your area:

Media Source	Contact Info: Key People	#People Reached	Information, history, etc.
Newspapers			
Commercial TV			
Cable TV			
Radio			
Newsletters			
College Media			
Other:			

Chapter Seven

Reinventing
Our Programs

The volunteer program administrator of today and the future will have to be an organizational engineer/architect and builder of the first order! She must acquire specific competency in this area and be willing to upgrade these skills as the years march on.

If you are not already re-shaping, re-designing or re-inventing your program, you may want to quickly begin to do so. Organizations, including their volunteer program, are re-inventing themselves constantly and the wiser ones understand that such current efforts will be obsolete within five years!

If you are enjoying smooth waters now because you have recently reshaped your efforts, take a deep breath, because in our fast-paced world of change, what works today will probably be less than adequate in a short time as needs change.

We can no longer come up with answers that last, because the questions keep changing!

Because of this, all of us must reshape the way we do business, re-engineering our volunteer programs and their efforts; restructuring who does what, where and when; readjusting our position in the larger institution and re-aligning our relationships.

Steve McCurley and I are in our second decade as business partners. In those years, we have re-invented ourselves several times, and how we do business today is very different from how we did business two, five or ten years ago.

We've even changed our name slightly. Originally we came up with a rather obvious name: **VMSystems**. Most people assumed that because we specialized in volunteer management services and products that that stood for "Volunteer **Management Systems**".

We did not try to correct anyone, even though that was an inaccurate assumption.

VMSystems has always stood for **Vineyard-McCurley** Systems, and as we have broadened what we do beyond the confines of volunteer management, we have changed our letter-head and business cards to the Vineyard-McCurley name.

It's a subtle change, but symbolic. Other changes were not so subtle.

We began with the short-term goal of marketing ourselves as national and international trainers with expertise in volunteer management issues. Our first book, "101 Ideas for Volunteer Programs" was our attempt to have people link our names together and to demonstrate the breadth of our knowledge in volunteerism so that we could generate more training and speaking dates. *At that point we were a Training company which offered publications on the side.*

Our mission was to produce services and goods to serve volunteerism; both were to be highly informational, easy to absorb, practical and even fun. We wanted to teach people how to become independent thinkers and problem-solvers, never dependent on others to feed them solutions. One relational "long-term goal" was to work ourselves away from having to be on the road constantly and to find a way to mentor other trainers/authors to serve the field.

Within two years of the start of our partnership, we established a publishers co-op, where we approached newer trainers and encouraged them to write a monograph for us in their expertise. Rather than the usual publisher's contract which gives the author 10% of sales after all expenses are paid, we offered these trainers 75% of all sales if they would pay for the printing of their booklet and up to $600 for the production and mailing of our catalogs in the year their book was printed. *At this point we shifted to being a Training/Publishing company.*

We offered these authors constant marketing and exposure plus referrals for training when people called us and were seeking someone with their specialization. We also helped them get their book camera-ready for the printer, arranged printing and proofing, stored their books, insured them against loss, processed orders, billed and collected from buyers, offered their books on consignment to conferences and reviewed them in our newsletter, GRAPEVINE.

As this part of our business grew to 15 authors, I accepted fewer on-the-road training jobs so that I could handle the increased administrative load this demanded. Steve stayed on the road and kept his eye out for potential new authors who might add needed topics to our growing Volunteer Marketplace Catalog. We started out with four titles and grew to over 70 at its peak! *At this point we were a Publishing/Training & Referral company.* We even offered a newsletter for trainers called "Training Wheels".

We also invited our authors to join us in a consortium-arrangement to offer support, cross-referrals and joint ventures to one another. As they became more independent and increased their individual visibility and reputations in the field (or decided to go in new directions), Steve and I backed away, feeling good about helping over a dozen trainers/authors grow professionally.

At this point we set new goals and shifted into being *a Consulting/Training & Publishing company,* seeking longer-term relationships with clients in which we could offer training, consulting and material-development on contract. We dropped the publishing co-op option from our menu, though we still carried our past author's products for at least one more year. We also began to concentrate heavily on our newsletter for volunteerism, GRAPEVINE, and changed its format from four to 16 pages, with full how-to articles that you would only expect to find in trade magazines. We dropped "Training Wheels" as a separate entity and folded it's content into Grapevine.

At each point of re-engineering we did an audit of where our time was being spent as well as our dollars and looked carefully at what the field needed. We came up with one over-riding demand: Good Information. Quickly!

With this as our guide we re-invented ourselves once again. I am basically off the road except for work with consulting clients and two major conferences a year; Steve is traveling between training and consulting clients and gathering information from the field we can share through Grapevine.

As relatively small as we are, an assessment told us that we needed to "out-source" two of our major efforts: the distribution and subscription monitoring of GRAPEVINE: Volunteerism's Newsletter, and the catalog and ordering process of our products. Thus another shift.

This change has freed me up to write more books, develop materials for clients and act as a central point for information among volunteerism's leaders. It allows Steve to concentrate on long-term consulting work and some speaking engagements. A far cry from where we began in the mid 1980s.

In the grand scheme of things, we are a tiny, tiny company, yet we have re-shaped ourselves five times, and will no doubt change several times again before we are promoted to the great trainer's room in the sky!

I've taken your valuable time to share all of this, because it's the example I know best that demonstrates re-shaping of an entity. Though the details will differ from your efforts to re-engineer your program, the concepts should remain the same:

☞   Look at what is needed.

☞   Look at what you're doing.

☞   Seek appropriate ways to realign the two.

☞   Let go of the old; embrace the new.

☞   Always keep an eye on your mission; it
      should be the driving force.

Re-shaping ourselves was rather easy for us because we only had to get "permission" from each other. Since we shared the same goal of meeting changing needs of the field, it took few discussions and short sentences. (Usually a 20 minute "annual meeting" over lunch at some conference or other!)

Your task may not be as easy. More people will need to be involved in assessing and planning for change; others will have to be convinced that the change is good; past innovators will have to be re-assured that changing what they once created does not reflect negatively on their contributions, and finally, the proper time for change will have to be targeted.

Re-inventing forces change on many who don't want to change. Many will go into a form of "culture shock" when it's forced on them....

......   Library volunteers who don't trust that a computer can hold as much
       information and be as easy to access as their familiar old card catalog.

......   Hospital auxillians used to making decisions independent of the
       authority of the director of volunteers.

...... Nursing home volunteers unafraid of direct contact with patient's bodily fluids and refusing to adhere to rules about protective gloves, masks and gowns.

...... Board member volunteers who for years made policy but were never before asked to raise funds.

...... Volunteer coordinators having to adhere to mandates from OSHA, the IRS' rule on unrelated income, the hospital's Joint Commission, the American With Disabilities Act, etc.

...... Board members dealing with issues of risk, liability, blood-borne pathogens, service-learning requirements, post-service credit issues, stipend-volunteers, mentoring guidelines or shifting funding.

Change is upon us. All of us will re-shape what we do several times in the next five years. Some will resist changing. They will be left in the dust.

Ask football historians.

Up to 1906 football was a game of kicking and running. Offensive strategy was limited mostly to seven men forming a wedge behind which the ball carrier ran. The object was to drive the defensive line back three or four yards so the ball could be advanced. It was a game of "four yards and dust".

In 1906 the forward pass was legalized. Most teams scoffed at the idea and stuck with their running game.

One team, St. Louis University, saw the pass as the wave of the future and re-shaped their game plans to use it extensively.

That year, St. Louis out-scored their opponents **402** to 11!

Any questions?

Re-Shaping. Where to Begin?

Like any re-shaping effort, it must begin with looking at where you are now. If you plan to re-shape yourself, the first step is a look in the mirror. (7-1)

For organizations, that means looking carefully at the assumptions we carry around with us and bring into the workplace. Each of us probably lug around more than we realize, and any one of them can be so strong that no one questions them. Such assumptions might include:

..... "Everyone knows who we are and what we do; it's obvious. We don't have to tell people about our work."

..... "Everyone knows that volunteers work here."

..... "We have lots of volunteers so we don't need to be concerned about recruitment."

...... "All our volunteers are XXXXXXX; anyone different would not fit in."

..... "We know what volunteers are "out there" for us to draw on."

..... "Our Board makeup will always remain the same."

..... "Our funding sources will continue as they have for years."

..... "The relationship we now have with our agency will always remain the same."

..... "Our clients need the same things we identified last year."

For many years, while I was going at my most frantic pace as a traveling trainer, I used a cartoon drawing that I would generate on a flip chart with audience participation. It showed the old, stereotypical volunteer....white, female, at-home mom and wife, well-educated, 50 hr/week volunteering.... which I named "Polly Do-Gooder" or "Volunteerus Extinctus".

I used this teaching method to help people examine (and discard) the old assumptions about who the typical volunteer was. I did this by comparing current statistics on who was really volunteering to the old assumptions.

In a broader context, but with a more specific view, all of us in volunteer leadership must examine our assumptions about volunteers in general and our individual programs specifically.

Call it an Assumption Audit and hold a brainstorming session with volunteers and paid staff plus other interested parties to create it. Soon. Establish a climate that allows people the peace of mind and freedom to share even the most bizarre or buried assumptions that they, or those they know, harbor.

Leave no stone unturned. Examine and list on a flip chart any assumptions around volunteers, your program, your larger agency, the Board, clients, funding and support, public perceptions, recruitment, recognition, etc. etc. Where-ever you can spot assumptions, dig them out and put them where everyone can see them to check them against reality.

Do not be surprised when people realize that they have totally different assumptions that they had never questioned. Do not let them stop during this first brainstorm session that uncovers assumptions; set rules at the beginning of your session that state that any discussions will be saved until after the first list is completed.

Your goal for naming as many assumptions as possible in this first session is to remove barriers to openness that might exist.

Next, categorize assumptions on different flip-chart sheets and then begin discussing the accuracy of those listed. Discuss how inaccurate or misguided assumptions can be erased; separate out those that your group considers accurate and begin examination of each by asking several key questions.

To share an example, let's pretend that a Director of Volunteers (DVS) in a hospital calls key staff and volunteers together to look at assumptions. (Most people would label some embedded assumptions as "truths", so be prepared to call them this.) They plan to look at the assumption that *volunteers can only work within the hospital walls/grounds.*

What are the consequences of believing this assumption?

> ....*Development of new programs is only focused on in-house services.*
> ....*There is a finite limit to the number of programs.*
> ....*People do not think of programs outside the hospital.*
> ....*Volunteers must come to the site.*

This thinking can lead to sub-assumptions such as:

> ...*It probably makes it easier to manage these programs.*
> ....*It is probably a rule of the administration.*

What do these assumptions impact?

> ....*Job designs.*
> ....*Recruitment.*
> ....*Planning.*
> ....*Response to needs outside of the hospital.*
> ....*Duties of DVS.*
> ....*Funding.*
> ....*Style of management and supervision.*
> ....*Creative solutions to some client's problems.*

What is the probable history behind this assumption?

> ....*Hospitals founded by volunteers centralized health care & tradition continued the pattern of centralization.*
> ....*Hospitals' mission was to heal the sick & help the lame.*
> ....*Hospital volunteering goes back to the days when wealthy women did "charity work" and found it both rewarding and socially pleasurable to work on a common cause with friends. .*
> ....*The tradition of on-site volunteering in hospitals has become a pattern.*
> ....*The belief that volunteer's job was to "keep the hospital doors open."*

What is the real mission of hospitals?

> ....*To promote & serve health and wellness needs of the community.*

What was/is the real mission of volunteers?

> ....*To assist the health care system in serving the community*

How is the hospital serving that mission now? What are plans for the future?

> ....*The hospital is now a wellness promoter with emphasis on prevention and education; in-hospital stays are costly for both patient and hospital; health care systems are using creative thinking to keep their programs operational with the hospital itself being just one of the programs.*

> ....*To be more visible in the community by offering off-site services, health-care, education and wellness.*

....To gain a wider base of support throughout the community.

....To be cost-effective.

What might the results be if this assumption (volunteers work on site) was laid aside?

....We could go to the administrators who are planning for the future and show them how volunteers could be a key part of any community out-reach programs they might be considering.

....The administration might see volunteer services as the logical link to the general public, to help the hospital identify needs, to build wider support within the population and to actually provide services.

....Enlightened executive staff would recognize the value of the natural contacts that volunteers have into the community churches, schools, organizations and neighborhoods which could be tapped in order that new programs might be more easily welcomed in those settings.

....A greater variety of jobs could be available for volunteers; this might attract a wider diversity and number of volunteers.

....If volunteers are asked to keep their eyes open and report back on needs in the community, the hospital can act on those reports,. This will allow them to help fulfill their obligation for community service as mandated by the IRS and local governments for nonprofit status.

....People who have volunteered for years or in the past but gotten bored with the available in-house jobs might be stimulated to rejoin the volunteer team as an active member with a new assignment.

Many of you might have come up with different assumptions or conclusions, depending on your own program, but this gives you an idea of where such a brain-storming session can lead. It's rather like an exercise in going outside the lines; of looking at issues up-side-down and in-side-out to inspire new perspectives.

Give a rubber mallet to a 2 year old. No one has ever told him what it's for and how to use it, so he looks at it from all angles, chews on the handle, sits on the mallet end, digs in the sand with it and pushes it around the floor like a truck. He has not been inhibited by anyone else's definitions or "truths", he simply has a new toy in his life that can **be** and **do** an amazing array of things.

The Power of "What If....?"

As you continually look at ways to reshape your program or organization you may wish to tap into the power found behind the words: "What if...?"

By modeling your own willingness to question assumptions and current practices, you will encourage others to do the same. (7-2)

Try putting a large sheet of paper on a wall in your office. In large block letters write "WHAT IF...?" at the top and invite everyone with an idea to jot down their thoughts. Give them the option of signing their name or keeping it anonymous.

Then, at regular intervals, gather a group of interested parties such as volunteers, staff, clients, etc. to discuss them. Insure that such discussions consider everything fairly; don't allow anything, no matter how far-fetched it might seem, to be dismissed without careful examination. Even the most outlandish idea might have a gold thread hidden somewhere!

In case you've never considered the power of "what if...?", join me in looking around. My Apple computers, phone, FAX and answering machines all remind me of the power of those words because they all began with one or two people saying "What if....?"

As we cope with the changes around us, we must find ways to release the child in those around us; having the courage to look at assumptions in innovative ways and stimulate creative thinking about productive new paths toward goals.

In the process, we may re-shape our programs and re-invent ourselves several times over while raising our competency levels to new heights.

In short, we will design programs and become people with more light bulbs drawn over our heads!

Assumptions

If any effort is to be reshaped, its current configuration must be carefully examined. It is a relatively simple task to review the organizational chart, budget, timelines, etc. to look for areas that might be streamlined or re-configured for greater effectiveness.

What is far more difficult than examining such tangible aspects is identifying and then examining intangible aspects of your organization or effort. The most critical, and difficult, exercise before reshaping can take place, is the honest examination of assumptions that exist. Every business has them, so do not dismiss this search as something that does not apply.

What Assumptions Existed When Your Organization or Program Began? What response was created related to each?
- Example: Assumption: Poor people have less than they need of basics of food, shelter, etc. Response: Salvation Army Programs to establish shelter to feed hungry, etc.

Which of the founding assumptions remain today? Which are still relevant? What programs exist that are still relevant?

What new assumptions have been added through time? Are they accurate?

What assumptions are held by the public? Clients? Volunteers? Paid staff? Funders? Other programs serving the same population?

What new assumptions might be added to enhance your work? Which assumptions should be discarded? How will this change the way you go about your work?

Reshaping

After the examination of assumptions and how work is currently done, how might processes, lines of authority, activities, interactions, etc. be redesigned to increase effectiveness?

What the organization* looks like now:

What it might look like if redesigned to be more effective:

Who would need to be involved in changes toward this new design:

Who would be impacted by such redesign? How? When?

Who would need to give their OK before such a change could be initiated?

*Substitute "program" or "effort" if you cannot impact the wider organization.

Chapter Eight

Broadening Your Resource Base

If volunteer programs are to march boldly in the 21st century, designed to withstand the pressures and demands it brings, they must be independently strong with resources and support of their own. This will only come when the leaders who oversee such programs have developed competencies in the areas of resource development, persuasion and strategizing.

If there is one typical cry I hear from leaders of such volunteer programs today, it is that they are constantly at the mercy of the decisions of others, either for funding, permission or regulation. Every year, they tell me, they wait with trepidation for others to decide their fate and listen, after the fact, to the reasons behind budget cuts or programmatic slashes.

That stance is passive and reactionary.

It's also the opening peal of the death knell for such programs.

In order for volunteer program leaders to try to oversee their own destiny, they will have to have two ingredients for surviving and even thriving: becoming part of decision-making and FRIEND-raising.

THE DECISION-MAKING CIRCLE

The first is the wisdom and determination to become part of the decision-making circles within their organization. Each of you will have to determine where that level of authority lies and who the players are that are in it.

I suggest you begin immediately to map out the sites and personnel around which critical planning and decisions are made. Who controls the budget? Priorities? Policy? Resources?

Work assignments? Community service? Image? etc. etc. What is the history of each of these key players? What makes them tick? How do they get rewarded or recognized?

Learn as much about each player as possible. If you don't know them personally, find those who do and ask for insight about them. How do they best take in information? By talking things through? By reading about it first and then discussing it? By having a great deal of data and numbers or by a simple overview to be filled in later? Do they prefer examples and on-site demonstrations of ideas or needs? Do they prefer to listen to people who manage workers or those actually doing the work? etc. etc.

Parallel to this fact-finding, think of ways to let authority figures know about the value of volunteers in your agency. Gather facts and figures, case studies and examples, and put these in front of critical decision-makers. You will find hundreds of ways to demonstrate how volunteer efforts have furthered your mission, goals, service to the community and public image. Volunteering is the heartbeat of service; the best human interest stories come through volunteer efforts.

Such stories and services translate into tangible rewards for the agency often through fund raising, both because national statistics that tell us volunteers give twice as much as non-volunteers to charity and through the personal client-services stories that persuade funders to support your work.

Everyone has personal motivations for working in agencies such as ours. Find out what decision-makers' reasons are and how you can support their efforts through volunteer services, if possible.

In other words:

☞ Identify decision-makers and how they learn best.

☞ Identify best approaches that will get their attention and respect.

☞ Make a priority of theirs a priority of yours.

☞ Help them be successful in attaining the mission of your agency.

☞ Give them constant, concrete examples of how volunteers feed success.

☞ Help them see how volunteers become a positive voice within the Community, spreading the good word about what the agency does and establishing a base for future support from those who hear the message.

☞ Offer concrete data about the value of volunteers at the national level; show them how volunteers have helped organizations retain non profit status, satisfy mandates of governing agencies, etc. Be specific.

☞ Find ways to thank key supporters publicly; arrange for them to be recognized within the circles that are most meaningful to them. Really supportive CEO's are few and far between; show yours off so he/she can become a role model!

☞ Find creative ways to force authorities to understand how increasingly valuable volunteers are as needs increase, funds shrink, support thins & times change.

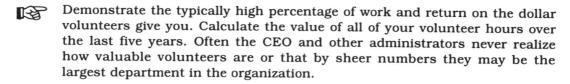 Demonstrate the typically high percentage of work and return on the dollar volunteers give you. Calculate the value of all of your volunteer hours over the last five years. Often the CEO and other administrators never realize how valuable volunteers are or that by sheer numbers they may be the largest department in the organization.

Do an overview of the work and decisions that volunteers and your program paid staff make. This has become a way for organizations to restructure salary and reward bases, and it can work in your favor to show how valuable your people, paid and non-paid, really are.

All of this, and the other important actions you will think of for your own particular situation, have a title. That title is "clout" and it is not a four-letter word. Clout is simply the honest accumulation of value and its documentation to others so that they respect all that you are and have to offer.

Clout is an energy force to use carefully, wisely, sparingly and directly to gain entry and earn a permanent place in the decision-making circles of your organization. It is also an energy that those in authority can tap to their advantage as they seek funds, look for support and garner recognition for their successes.

Positive clout is never used to abuse, threaten or coerce. It is used positively to leverage success and produce effectiveness in attaining the vision of the parent agency and the volunteer program which serves that vision.

In the hands of the competent, visionary servant-leader, clout is simply another word for empowerment, and a critical ingredient for success.

FRIEND-RAISING

A second ingredient of that same success is the main focus of this chapter....typically called FUND-RAISING.

It's a terrible word. Stop using it!

"Fund-raising" conjures up visions of going door to door and being rejected by typically sweet neighbors who bash you over the head with their broom for having the audacity to "beg" from them. It elicits visions of standing on street corners or in shopping malls with a picture of some pitiful creature rubber-banded onto a collection can as you plead with people to donate a coin or two.

Worse yet, the word *fund-raising* instantly says "rejection" to most people as they see themselves asking others for money and being turned down flatly.

No wonder asking for money is ranked at the top of the list of things adults want to avoid most, right below the most dreaded "public speaking" that is often part of fund-raising!

Let's make a pact that from now on, the word FUND-raising will never slip from between our lips again! Instead, let me suggest another word that changes the dynamics of acquiring resources and hopefully changes our attitude:

FRIEND-Raising.

Friend-raising: The User-Friendly Approach to Resource Development

Look what happens when you shift from FUND-raising to FRIEND-raising as a base for acquiring resources:

⇨ Fund-raising says "Success comes in getting money; the more the better."

Friend-raising says "Success comes from establishing a relationship."

⇨ Fund-raising puts the power in the hands of the person being asked.

Friend-raising shares the power between asker and asked.

⇨ Fund-raising typically means that if you are turned down, you don't go back.

Friend-raising means you can return.

⇨ Fund-raising limits efforts to money.

Friend-raising allows for many ways to connect and support one another.

⇨ Fund-raising says that if you get no money you have failed.

Friend-raising says that a "no" to a specific request does not mean failure. There are many ways to meet needs that do not involve dollars.

⇨ Fund-raising is not something most people like to do.

Friend-raising offers the possibility of relationships; it is rarely rejected.

⇨ Fund-raising sounds improbable at least and often impossible.

Friend-raising sounds possible.

In actuality, FRIEND-raising is the art of establishing a relationship with someone (or a corporate body) that can be mutually beneficial.

It establishes a base from which can be drawn a variety of resources including support, information, funds, goods, services, networking, expertise, and a rich tapestry of collaborative efforts. The truly good news is that these resources can go both ways within the relationship. It's actually a variation of **leader-shift,** most appropriately labeled "friend-shift" and can be extended to others through joint efforts.

The secret to successful friend-raising is a commitment to giving as much as you are getting: making the relationship mutually beneficial so that everyone involved feels they are receiving something of value for their time and effort.

The late Speaker of the U.S. House of Representatives, Tip O'Neil of Massachusetts, often reminded people of the great lesson his father had taught him about politics, by saying that:

"All politics are local."

The wisdom, Speaker O'Neil liked to point out, was that people are concerned with whatever affects them; what is closest at hand or in their own backyard.

It is as true in our field as it is in politics.

People are concerned with what affects them. If what you are asking touches something that is of interest or benefit to those you ask, you will have a better chance to get their involvement.

We've known this forever. Parents are deeply involved in PTA while their children are in school, but drop out of sight when those children move on. In the same pattern, parents volunteer to help to teach church school, work for the athletic boosters organizations, lead Scout troops, provide transportation, funds and all manner of help to Little League efforts and endure tortures beyond imagination on various field trips, campouts and class picnics simply because their little darlings are participating.

If you've ever doubted where their loyalty lies, try asking them to go on a January campout in Minnesota when their children are NOT involved and see how far you get.... only the terminally daft or those with some other personal desire for such a trip will embrace your invitation.

To implement friend-raising, therefore, you must have an ability to look at what you need and then decide what you might offer in exchange to anyone who is able to provide that need.

The concept of the exchange of value for value sounds rather simple, but I find it eludes most people. If friend-raising is to succeed, it must not only be understood, but carried out in actions that support its underlying principle of trading value for value, an exchange that speaks to partnering rather than begging.

Four Steps Toward Friend-raising

For those of you who have read my book "Marketing Magic", you are about to have a little refresher course, as the four steps in sound marketing are also the same steps in putting friend-raising into action.

Let's begin by looking again at the dreaded FUND-raising and its characteristics:

When people think of fund-raising they tend to begin with figuring out what dollars are needed, then moving on to who might give you those dollars, how to convince potential donors to say "yes" and how to thank donors appropriately.

Such an approach puts the asker at the mercy of the asked. A "no" stops the process and brands it a failure. It is often quick but never painless. Further pressure to get a "yes" typically angers the asked and brands the asker as "pushy" or obnoxious. Not exactly the start of a beautiful friendship.

FRIEND-raising, by comparison, has a very different approach. Its' four-step process looks like this:
   1. What do you HAVE? (What of value might you exchange with others.)

2. What do you NEED? (Specifically. Accurately. Needs, not less critical Wants.)
3. Who HAS what you need? (Identifying potential sources.)
4. HOW can you GET what you need? (Options of strategizing a trade of values.)

Take particular note of where this process begins. Unlike the process for fund-raising, it does not begin with *your* need, but what you already have that you might offer to others in exchange for what you need. The focus, therefore, is on a potential relationship and what others might value, not just on *your* need.

This first step establishes a pattern of concern for others. It also broadens the thinking of paid staff and volunteers involved with resource development, as it does not limit the definition of resources to money alone. Instead it tracks all the different assets your organization or program already has.... an exercise that can often lift the spirits of those believing that they are "too poor to carry on."

Step #1: *What Do You Have?*

Through brainstorming with others, create a list of what assets you have. Do not allow any idea to be "shot down" as it is offered. To assist participants creating such a list to focus on resources you already have, you might suggest categories such as tangible and intangible, people and things, etc. One of the worksheets at the end of this section suggests others.

Most organizations, after compiling such an inventory, are typically rejuvenated by seeing just how rich they already are. If their leader has the wisdom to put this list where everyone can see it, the number of items often grows as people think of new things to add to it.

Consider your own program and what it has in the way of:

Experts	Experience	Contacts	Networks	Information
Equipment	Supplies	Office space	Location	Trainings
Books & Tapes	Leaders	History	Clout	Education
Reputation	Resumé items	Clients	Volunteers	Social life
Tradition	Staff	Skill building	Teamwork	

Any one of the categories you consider can suggest hundreds of sub-categories that might hold things of value to others when trying to establish an exchange relationship. (8-1)

☞ ...The community club able to help supply workers for a special effort you plan might be desperate to have a more efficient computerization of its member roster. You could exchange after-hour use of your computer and a staff volunteer to help supervise the input of data. A trade of value for value.

☞ ...A local utility seeks a better community image as a caring & concerned neighbor. You suggest an insert in their monthly bill to consumers that highlights their workers helping your clients and the company's willingness to match donated time with dollars to the agency.

☞ ...A local bank is trying to be the "number one bank in the village." A new community service club wants greater visibility so that they might increase their membership. You suggest that the service group provide volunteers to sit in the lobby of the bank during the last week of every month to accept payments from citizens needing renewal of their license plates. The fee usually charged by the bank to cover this service is donated to your program. The license plates all have identifying letters that tell the community that the car's owner supported your program.

Everybody wins.....

...the publicity tells more people about your program services, and....

...associates your good reputation for service with the bank and the community group, and...

...gives you an on-going cash flow from the banks donations, and....

...tells people about the new service group, and...

...offers the club chances to recruit new folks as they buy their license plates, and...

...brings the bank great PR and a flow of potential customers through their doors, and..

...allows the bank to offer license services without taking staff away from their primary duties, and....

...serves as an "ad" for volunteers for your organization, and....

...serves the clients who reap the benefits of your program.

Charting what you might offer others in a trade relationship is only the beginning of the work implied by friend-raising's first step: What do you HAVE? You will also want to gather as much information as possible about the needs, characteristics and the dynamics of the population around you.

Additionally, you will need to look at what you have in the way of data and information that may shape your needs in the future. Look at demographics for your community.... what is the average age of your population? What income? Patterns of giving & volunteering? Energy level? Tradition? History? Associations? Networking? Attitudes? Languages? (See worksheet, Chapter 1-4.)

Who has traditionally supported you in the past? What people? Groups? Churches? Media? Governing bodies? Who has opposed you? Why? When? Over what issues? What common grounds do you currently have with either supporters or non-supporters? (8-2)

What power bases exist that must be dealt with? Who are they? What is their history with your organization? Do they have power over you? How? Why? When? What connection do you share with them? What mutual friends do you share? How can they be influenced? (8-3)

My list could go on an on. Consider this first step an audit of what and who you have around you that might be of value in your quest for support. Keep in mind that at the base of all that you consider, there are two guiding principles:

1. Ethical behavior.
2. A genuine desire to have all involved be a "winner".

This means that everything you do in examining or offering what you have is done without any thought of coercion, arm-twisting, implied threats or subversiveness. It is above-board and honest and is always in tune with your mission and vision. It is not part of score keeping that might lead to: "You turned me down last month so I'm turning you down today" thinking.

In offering what you have there is never a thought of masking anything with misinformation or, worse yet, DIS-information. Information is not withheld or over-emphasized. It is not slanted or prejudiced; it never degrades anyone or derides similar efforts.

When your friend-raising efforts are rooted in such ethical behavior and concern for others, the subsequent exchange relationships that follow are off to a good start, as they say to others: "I care as much about what you will get out of our relationship as I do about what I will get from it."

And that, my friend, is what friend-raising is all about.

When you are seeking a supportive or partnering relationship with an organization, you will consider the same factors as you do with individuals:

> ....what can I offer them that they value?
> ....what is of value to them?
> ....how can I insure that they benefit from their supportive relationship with us?

Keep in mind that most organizations have a reward system that is meaningful to them and probably comes from some higher authority. Whether a group is working for awards, public recognition or national acclaim, find out their system of reward and identify ways that their support of your needs can help them attain their honors.

One of the most valuable pieces of information that you can gather about an organization is its mission statement. Begin a file on key groups in your community and continue to add data about each. Identify leadership, affiliations, vision, history, projects, calendar, award system, authority and regulatory information, community visibility and reputation, structure, financial aspects, future plans, ambitions, etc. (8-4).

Ask those around you to add contacts and any information they might have about each group so that you have a rich resource file waiting to be tapped when an opportunity comes along to work together. Such a Resource File becomes more valuable each year.

The first step of Friend-raising, "What do you HAVE?", is critical to successful resource development for money, support, people, energies or things. It is the equivalent to checking your bank account to see what you have before you go out to buy anything.

Too often groups begin with "What do I need?", and then find themselves suffering from resource-myopia, the inability to recognize what they already have that can be used to get what they need. Instead, it is best to inventory your resources in a relaxed manner, unpressured by demands, by having everyone involved draw up a list of assets that can be part of future exchange relationships.

This "inventory" can also reveal out-of-date practices that no longer meet current realities. Such realizations of needs in life today are the reasons that hospitals have changed from sickness to wellness centers, that libraries shifted from being in the book business to the information business and that museums have gone from being storehouses of relics to centers for learning.

Step #2: *What do You NEED?*

Step number two, "What do you NEED?", can seem to be the most simple of the four steps, but is actually not as easy as it might seem.

I have worked with many groups through the year that didn't really "get" this critical step and couldn't figure out why they were bringing in less and less resources each year.

As I quizzed them about what they needed and why, they gave me answers like, "We need to grow" or "We need support for our field work." When I would try to pin them down to specifics, they were quite vague and a whole lot of guessing seemed to be going on.

As I probed to find out how figures were arrived at, they typically told me that department heads had simply increased their numbers from the year before. Until I got beneath vague references and convinced them that I really wanted specifics about how the money would be spent and who would benefit from the expenditure, they did not really catch on to how important Step #2 is in friend-raising.

They had not really understood that requests for support of any kind need to demonstrate:

> 1. A *specific* need.... and....
> 2. a direct benefit to the *clients served* by the group.

Thus, the Resources Department is not just asking for money to buy a new computer, it needs money to help keep track of people who will help the children stricken with (disease).

When dealing with the critical issue of what you NEED, you must be as specific as possible and tie your need to helping the people your cause serves. This can be difficult for some groups who have not clearly identified their "clients." For programs that serve sick children, poor families, abused spouses or troubled teens this exercise may seem a ridiculous waste of time, but for others, who the client is can be illusive. (See worksheets 8-5 and 8-6.)

Arts programs rarely see the people that come to their programs as "clients". They overlook the school children who benefit from having a "picture lady" come to their classroom and share the beauty and struggle of the artist of the various paintings. They forget that the art they hang in the subway station or mount in the park offers passersby a moment of beauty and peace, and in so doing, establishes a client relationship with them.

Program workers in recreation rarely label those that benefit from their efforts as clients just as churches forget that "member" is simply another word for "client". Volunteers who staff a surgical waiting room in a hospital or a waiting room in a free clinic often overlook the fact that the people they soothe and comfort there are every bit as much a "client" as the person receiving medical attention.

To create a clear picture of WHO will be served through a specific resource acquisition, the client must be kept foremost in the minds of those describing their need to others. Frankly, it is also a great way to measure whether something is truly needed or not: if attaining a goal does not serve the client, is it really needed?

Wants versus Needs

When using such a measuring stick, many groups have dropped some "needs" from their lists and seen them more appropriately for what they are: Wants.

Distinguishing between wants and needs is critical as you hone in on what must be present to accomplish your mission and what other things are really just icing on the cake. It is also critical to our Step #2 in Friend-raising.

Needs are those things that *must* be present for you to carry out your mission. Such a list would include things like office space, paid and volunteer staff, phones, computers and basic office equipment, specific skills or expertise, etc. etc.

Wants are those things that might make your work easier, more pleasant, even more efficient, but not having them would not force you to close your doors.

Keep in mind also that some things may move from one list to the other. For example, a staff retreat would normally be put on the "wants" list, but if a crisis develops among the staff and without clarification would cause people to leave your program, such a retreat moves from being a "want" to being a "need".

The trick is, as usual, to use common sense and constantly re-evaluate needs, using the same principles behind Leadershift which allow you to be flexible and responsive to changing dynamics.

Identifying any need can lead to a very complex exercise in thinking through the best ways to achieve a goal. It is never easy and rarely simple.

When we apply the concept of Friend-raising we also expand our thinking beyond money to resources of people, support, information, publicity, etc. Let's look at an example of all of this expanded thinking:

A historical museum has seen it's attendance drop over the past year. Its funding has also gone down because long-time Patrons have retired and moved away, younger supporters are not joining the Patron ranks and donations offered at the door have diminished because of poor attendance. A consultant is called in to diagnose what has happened and concluded that the founding Patrons, who had established the museum 30 years before, had given little attention to on-going publicity and recruitment of supporters based on their assumption that everyone "knows about our little museum; they'll come to us if they're interested."

The concerned Board of Directors decides it needs to devise a two-year plan to turn their fortunes around. Several needs are identified, including:

1. A speakers bureau that can provide speakers for local churches and groups and describe what the museum has to offer;

2. A process/system for scheduling and heavily publicizing working demonstrations of old world crafts at the museum during the Founder's Day celebration:

3. A traveling exhibit of interesting artifacts from the museum that will be offered at schools;

4. A video and book on the history of the town, and

5. A means for forging working partnerships with the Chamber of Commerce, Library Board, downtown Retail Merchants Association and other community groups that help promote the town's attractions.

Please note that no real fund-raising event is planned!

The traveling exhibit to schools takes high priority because it can reach so many people at once and surveys show that when children express an interest in a museum, parents are typically delighted to bring them to it.

To create the traveling exhibit several things are needed:

#1....Research to put together those stories and items regarding the town's history that would be of interest to grade school children.

#2....Someone to script the presentation, gather the artifacts and create the traveling exhibit.

#3.... Contact with school officials as to how best to offer the exhibit and its accompanying moderators who can share the stories with the children and then answer questions they might have. Assemblies? In individual or joint classroom settings? At school fairs?

#4.... Selection and training for the volunteers who will present the exhibition.

#5....Creation of graphics needed to accompany the exhibit; also possible costumes for the moderators. (The arts world often calls such people "Interpreters")

#6.... Funds for creation and transport of the exhibition; a realistic budget.

#7.....Someone to write about the exhibition and share it with local media.

#8.....A means to evaluate efforts.

Keep in mind that all of these eight needs or objectives are sub-categories under one of the major needs identified at the start of the museum's thinking: *a school-focused traveling exhibit.* By clearly identifying each you can then move on to step number three in friend-raising: WHO HAS what you need?

The process shown in the example above is really a rather simple one...

 Start with a problem;

...Break the problem down & restate it in the form of a goal;
...Identify options for attaining the goal;
...Break each option down into manageable steps;
...Assign each step to appropriate people;
...Take action.

Typically, in mapping out all the actions that go into making up such a need, people come to mind that might help with each goal and objective. The more this occurs, and the more each objective suggests several specific people, the greater your chances of finding the right person for each job.

Too often, needs remain unmet because we have not broken our thinking down into small enough parts that people can handle. Think about the difference between asking one person to help get media publicity for the traveling exhibit and asking one person to do everything required to create and carry off a "traveling exhibit for all the schools in town".

The first, smaller request seems possible, the second feels overwhelming! In our world when time and energy are the most coveted "currencies" of life, asking people to do things that would take mountains of time and work is the quickest route to a big fat "NO"; asking them to do something that will take a small amount of time, little energy and is spread over a wide calendar puts you much closer to the desired "yes".

Step #3: *WHO HAS What You Need?*

As you map out the specifics of your goals and objectives, you are beginning to sketch out a picture of who might be the right person to make each action happen.

Going back to the example of the traveling exhibit for schools and looking at the eight objectives outlined, a thoughtful brain-storming session will probably draw out suggestions of people for each objective. Sometimes the suggestions will be specific people by name, such as John Smith, Nancy Clark, etc. At other times there will be suggestions that revolve around a position...the principals at the grade schools, one of the editors of the local newspaper, etc., and still other suggestions will describe characteristics needed for the assignment such as "someone with adult training skills", "an artist", etc.

At this point the Resource File mentioned in Step #1 becomes invaluable. In it you would find names of people and groups who might be called on to do the necessary work. For example, you may not personally know an artist who could create the graphics for the exhibit, but you have the name of the local arts group in the file and a quick call to their president may help you come up with a specific name.

Addressing the question of WHO HAS what you need is simply the next logical step in achieving your goal. By generating the names of many people who might accomplish the identified objective, you have a greater chance of meeting your need. (8-7)

By breaking down needs into the smallest manageable parts you also have increased your chances for success by avoiding the deadly "over-load" on volunteers that burns them out quickly. Volunteers today have so many demands for their time and energy that potential burnout can come very quickly as they already are on overload when they come to you.

There is no greater resource available to you than people. When you involve a maximum number, give them smaller jobs that are clearly defined and then help them achieve success, you are widening your resource base dramatically and building a foundation for the future.

In other words: FRIEND-raising!

C. 1996 S. Vineyard. STOP MANAGING VOLUNTEERS!

Step #4: *HOW Do You GET What You Need?*

The last step in widening your resource base through Friend-raising addresses how you get each identified person that you want to join your effort.

It is the strategizing part of your Friend-raising effort where you look back to the list you generated in Step #1 of resources and valuable assets you have that you might exchange for each individual's involvement. (8-8)

Remembering that your goal is to trade whatever you have to offer for the help of the people you want to recruit, you now begin to think through what you might offer each person that would provide an equitable exchange for you and them.

Keep in mind that you must juggle three objectives in your effort:

1. You need to have the work done.

2. You want recruits to get as much or more out of the relationship as you do.

3. You are trying to establish a good relationship that goes beyond the immediate assignment and even survives a person turning this request down!

There may be no stronger point at which we can see the difference between fund-raising and friend-raising more clearly that in the third objective listed above. A "no" in a fund-raising effort often ends the interaction. In friend-raising, however, it is simply part of the on-going relationship and does not signal any "end."

If a person turns down your request for help you can still keep them informed about your effort, invite them to a special event where they will come in closer contact with your program, seek their advice on future efforts, etc. All of these options simply continue the relationship, keeping the person as a FRIEND to you and your program.

In planning your approach to individuals, I urge you to brainstorm all of the benefits you could offer them. Then decide to WHOM you have the most to offer and target them for your recruitment appeal. The Arts Club may give you the name of a graphic artist who could provide the art work needed for the museum's traveling exhibit but so can the Technical College in town. *That* person could get a greater benefit from your relationship because the work can be part of their resumé, it offers them exposure to many people in the community who might hire them, gives them practical experience and credit at the college. You'd be wise to first ask such a person, because you have the most to offer in exchange for his/her doing your artwork.

I would like to add four points on increasing your rate of successful enlistment:

⮕ *Carefully choose WHO you assign to recruit specific people to help you.*

People are more likely to say "yes" to someone they know or respect. Your resource file should tell you about personal contacts, so search there for someone who might already have a connection to those you want to enlist.

Plan the timing of your request carefully.

Avoid high-stress or work-overload times in peoples lives. Asking a working mother of three just before Christmas to help you in February, will probably get you a resounding "NO!" because she is so overloaded with holiday details and hyperactive children waiting for Santa. Asking her in January when that is all behind her would probably be wiser and more successful.

 Be specific and target your approach.

Be specific on what you want them to do. Tell them how long you need their help and what support you can offer them. It they have an interest that is touched by the job you need to be done target your approach accordingly.

When trying to recruit a retired teacher to help with the traveling museum exhibit, for example, stress the educational benefit. If you are talking to a life-time resident, talk about the benefits of children appreciating the town's heritage, etc.

As you work to recruit people to tasks, clearly outline the support they will have and the expected results of the work.

 Never promise what you can't deliver.

NEVER promise them help you won't be able to give them and NEVER set up expectations that are unrealistic.

ASKING

This final step in friend-raising draws all your previous planning together as background to this strategize the most critical phase, the *asking*. As much as you have used this skill in the past, the demands of today require you to rise to a new level of competency in the art of persuasion, to equal the increasing reluctance of people to "take on one more thing."

You will move toward the asking stage of Step #4 by creating a Friend-raising Action Plan.

This plan (see worksheet 8-8 at end of chapter) outlines:

1. The major people that have or can acquire what you need.

2. What you might offer each as an exchange for that need.

3. Who might be the most likely to be successful in approaching each.

4. When might be the best timing for an approach.

5. General background information.

6. The specifics of what you will ask for and how you will ask.

When all of this is outlined, you will make a judgment as to who would be the most likely to respond positively to your request. My personal bias is to aim toward those for which you have the most to offer in an exchange.

Decide which person you will approach first; then rank all the others in descending order. This creates a mindset that says, "we do not have only one option, there are many."

In creating your approach, keep in mind several key points:

☞ You are not trying to talk anyone into saying "yes", but instead, trying to remove their reasons to say "no."

   ...As you discuss your need, be clear, concise and direct. People tend to say no when they are unclear as to what you want them to do.

   ...Tell them what you need and why. People give to people, so explain how meeting your need will help clients. People want their time and resources to be used wisely and make a difference in PEOPLE terms.

   ...People fear failure, un-ending assignments, and lack of control. Be specific in telling them how success will be measured, any past history, your support of them, how much time it will take and what controls are in place to direct actions effectively.

   ...If they raise objections, diagnose what their root fear is and remove the objections. If someone raises an objection you cannot remove ("I don't want to work with anyone from the suburbs.") be honest with them, remembering that you never promise what you can't deliver!

☞ There are two basic reasons that people give their resources of time, energy, money or gifts:

   #1...*They feel they will get something of value in return for their involvement.*

The returned value might include:

   A. Personal issues: (parenthesis suggests groups which might tap this value)

      ..."You helped me or a loved one once." (schools)

      ..."I/a loved one might need you one day." (hospital, ambulance service)

      ..."This allows me time with loved ones." (church clean-up project)

      ..."I can model good behaviors to my kids." (homeless shelter on a holiday)

      ..."I feel I am making a difference." (Aids program)

      ..."This helps me build my resume." (church treasurer)

      ..."Helps me make new contacts." (Rotary Club)

..."Allows me to enjoy a hobby. (Historical Society)

"It's FUN!" (event planning)

B. Belief systems:

"It promotes my values." (family life programs)

"It's patriotic." (4th of July parade)

"It allows me to put my faith into action." (programs for homeless)

"It allows me to put my beliefs into action." (political campaign)

"I can act on my family tradition of volunteering." (library program)

C. Safety issues:

"It will help my community be safer." (crime-prevention program)

"It will keep my town be economically strong." (downtown renovation)

"It preserves the future." (environmental programs)

"It protects my future." (new ambulance service)

"It helps me stay healthy." (sports & wellness programs)

"It gives my business publicity." (walkathon support)

This list could go on and on, to include tangible and intangible rewards, very altruistic and less altruistic rewards, temporary and permanent values (to be honest, I only worked on the PTA board when our sons were in school; after that, I was out of there! .... a temporary value.) and those very specific to an individual's experience.

Film actor Christopher Reeve is a classic example of this individualized support. After his riding accident in 1995 and his paralysis, he became an outstanding spokesperson for the issue of spinal cord injury. Asking him to help that cause became an "easy sell" as he was determined to do all he could to help others understand the range and plight of people with such injuries and the need to direct funding toward research to help victims.

#2: The second reason people respond positively to requests for assistance is a commitment or tie to the asker.

Therefore, the teacher is more likely to say "yes" to a request for help if a student assists in the asking process; a parent is more likely to agree when their child asks, and an individual is most likely to respond positively when asked by a friend, etc.

Choose the asker carefully. If it is one who the potential giver knows, cares about and trusts, you are probably going to get a "yes." If you don't know the person to be asked personally, take along or ask for the help of someone they do know.

          C. 1996 S. Vineyard. **STOP MANAGING VOLUNTEERS!**

Such a third party is called an "authenticator" and can be invaluable in helping you gain access to, gather information about, and plan the best approach to a targeted person or group.

How you ask is also important...understand that the most effective method is in person, one on one (or two on one if you take along an authenticator). The next best is in-person to multiple potential recruits, such as in a presentation to a club or group of employees. The third choice would be over the phone and the least effective is via mail, especially if the person on the other end of your appeal does not know you or your cause. These last two options, telemarketing and direct mail, are intended to blitz a gazillion people in the hopes of getting one or two percent to respond. It's better to spend your time researching and approaching targeted individuals.

Friend-raising is at the root of good resource development. It helps us look beyond money to the other resources we'll all need to keep our efforts going strong into the new century.

The wider and more diverse we can make our resource base, the better we will be. This can only happen if we increase our competencies toward involving as many people as possible in our efforts and make them feel good about our working relationships.

With such a broad base of support, the volunteer program leader will probably be able to meet every challenge and survive every change that comes along!

What Do You Have?

List assets you have. Include things such as money, equipment, people, contact, expertise, programs, goods, services, information, site, network, supplies, location, trainings, publications, leaders, clout, reputation, clients, staff, volunteers, tradition, skill building, vision, social contacts, etc..   .....anything you might be willing to trade for needs in the future.

Support

List key people and groups who have supported you in the past. What is your current relation with each?

Power Bases

As suggested in the teaching text of this book, what power bases exist that must be dealt with? Who are included? What is their power over you? What history do they have with you? How can they be persuaded to support you?

Resource File Inventory

Name of Group: Today's date:
                                                (Revise each time updated)
Leadership (update regularly):   Size of Group:

Contact address/phone:

Mission statement or purpose:

Founded:_____(date)_____(founders)

Brief History:

History of interaction w/your organization: (update regularly)

Structure & Governance: (part of national group? Board? etc.)

How funded?   Do they fund others? Who/What?

General Information:

Contacts you have with or to them:

What Do You Need?

Need	Why?	When Need?	How related to mission?	#Priority

Who Are Your Clients?

Who do you serve?   How?

Who are also served? Example: You serve sick kids; when they are helped their parents benefit, too.

Who Has What You Need?

Need	Who has?	What needs do they have, you might offer in trade?

Getting What You Need!

Need	Who Has?	Trade you offer?	Who best Contact?	Timing	Approach & Info:

Chapter Nine

The Role of
Change Agent

When we look at the competencies that volunteer program leaders of any title must have, we have to look at how much change they will have to deal with during their tenure and the ways they will manage the changes rather than be managed by them.

When we accept the role of an entrepreneur, as we discussed in a previous chapter, we also are accepting the role of being a change agent, one who brings change about.

Let's start by agreeing that that is easier said than done.

Someone once said that the only constant in life is change. That is especially true in the volunteer arena as our work is based on responding to needs each day. Unlike companies that sell soap and only need to be aware of buyer's patterns, we in volunteerism are trying to juggle changing needs of clients, potential clients, volunteers, paid staff, funders, administrators, governing bodies and the general public. Add to this, changing mandates and information from courts, regulatory agencies, societal trends and values and you can understand why volunteer program leaders confess to high stress on the job.

In all of this your job is to stay calm, adjust and be as effective as possible. Volunteers and staff need it, the public demands it, administrators expect it and your clients deserve it. "It" of course is your very best efforts, each day, every day.

If that Herculean task is to happen, you must be equipped with an ability to deal with change and in fact, be a change agent: one who anticipates, causes, manages, controls and directs change as required for success.

Understanding Change

Change is a shift from what was to what must newly be. It means you start at one point and move to another. It requires an ability to map a course from the present to the future with minimum casualties and maximum speed. It demands that you help others and yourself to "let go" of what was so that you can embrace the new.

As your program's primary change agent, it is up to you to make change as smooth as possible. To do this, you have to understand that people will resist change when:

☞ They believe it will reduce their authority or position.

☞ They believe it will disrupt their established work patterns.

☞ They believe it will be forced without their input.

☞ They believe it will reduce or eliminate the options they now enjoy.

☞ They believe it will force them into work that they cannot handle.

☞ They believe it will reduce their opportunities to interact with significant others.

☞ They believe it will take away some securities they currently have.

☞ They believe it will reduce their rewards.

☞ They believe it is being done to punish or embarrass them.

☞ They believe it will be forced on them at times of high stress & other demands.

From your own experiences, you may be able to add to this list. Its purpose is to simply help you think through any potential objections you might encounter as you introduce change. Knowing how people might resist changes will help you strategize the reduction of this resistance and possibly suggest allies you will want to have help you bring the change about. (9-1)

Here are some suggestions on how to cut down or even eliminate resistances:

#1: Understand that you are going to be dealing with people who fear loss.... loss of prestige, position, friends, familiar work routines, relationships, rewards, success. It will be your challenge to help them overcome those fears. To do so, you will want to:

...Keep people informed as the change is planned; show time frames when possible.

...Spell out specifically how the change will or will not impact work, people, etc.

...Detail how people will be rewarded after the change is in place.

...Listen honestly to people's expressed fears; never dismiss them as foolish. You are dealing with people's feelings, which to them, are facts. Listen carefully and address each fear directly and with as few words as possible. Avoid "over-talking" any response; be concise in order to reduce any later misinterpretation of what you said.

...If you are changing a process or structure, have someone draw it on a chart so that visual learners can "see" how the change will work.

...Assume the good intentions of everyone; draw on their concern for your clients and show them how the new change will more directly benefit the client.

...Explain the reason for change; be sure it's valid. Relate it to your mission.

...Detail how people will be trained and equipped to handle new responsibilities.

#2: Keep in mind that you may be dealing with some people who were part of creating the older entity you are now changing; they may feel "ownership" of the old and wounded personally that you think it is no longer "good". Help them to see that:

... The new change is built on the old; if the old had not been there, the new could not have been possible.

... Recognize such people for their contribution. Remind them that when they first brought it about, IT was the new change!

... If an old idea or activity is being dropped completely, celebrate all the good it did in its lifetime. Brainstorm and put on a large flip chart all of the benefits it brought to your program. If you have a strong and positive climate, you may even be able to list challenges it also brought that will not be missed.

... Find creative ways to recognize founders of efforts now being changed. If your program is a large one with a lot of newer volunteers and paid staff, you might feature an article in your newsletter or on your bulletin board letting everyone know who helped formulate efforts originally. Possibly a "Who helped to start our gift shop?" contest that involves volunteers in looking at the history of your efforts.

#3: Accept the fact that not everyone can be happy about the changes.

... Do not let your goal stray toward wanting to make everyone happy. That's not practical or possible. Simply believe in your change, introduce it carefully and direct its application. You will lose some people who simply cannot accept it. Bid them farewell, thank them for all that they have done, expect that they will take some of their friends with them and get back to your role as change agent.

#4: Look around for people who can help you make the changes. Identify those people others look to for guidance and leadership. Find out where they stand and ask them for their help in implementing the change.

... Reward those who help you make the change possible.
... Ask these helpers to speak to others about the good in the change.
... Ask them to share with you new concerns and suggestions of how to overcome them.
... Listen to their advice as the change is planned and implemented.
... Listen to them as they suggest fine-tuning needed as the change is implemented.

... Ask for their assistance in enlisting other leaders to help make the change happen.

... Involve them in assessing how well the change process worked and how well the change itself is working. Can either be improved? How?

Keep in mind that you are never trying to twist arms to get people to say "yes" to the change, you are simply trying to remove their reasons to say no to it. And if that sounds like something you have heard from me before in this book and others, you are correct.... it is a guiding principle of persuasion and friend-raising!

The primary job of a change agent is to have the capability of identifying needed change, designing and introducing it and drawing in those effected by it so that they can become advocates and successful workers as it is implemented. People want to be involved in changes that effect them. They do not want to be fearful about change, but be reassured that it is in their or the client's best interests. These desires are as human as any in our world, and it is the change agent that recognizes this and brings both the people and change about smoothly and safely. (9-2; 9-3; 9-4)

A new competency and a critical one.

The Change Agent and the Brick-Wall Syndrome

I suspect that in every change agent's life they can recall a moment when they had a bright idea about which they were so excited they could hardly stand it. They took the idea to a significant other, with arms flailing and eyes sparkling, and explained their revelation with words tumbling over one another, then stood back and waited for the listener to jump up and down, clapping with glee and cheering their brilliance!

...And they waited and they waited and they waited and then listened as the other person dismissed the idea as silly, foolish, impossible, impractical or with that dreaded spirit-killing word, "no".

It was as that point, whether age 5 or 55 that they first felt their heart drop to their toes, their breath leave their body and their mouth drop open in absolute shock and bewilderment. If they could find their voice it probably sounded foreign as they replied, "huh?".

It's a shock to a person's entire being when they run into a brick wall of rejection regarding an idea they though held the answer to the mysteries of the universe! And it hurts, too. The seemingly inarticulate response of "huh?" sums up a melting pot of questions, disbelief and shock:

1. "But it's a great idea...."
2. "Let me explain....."
3. "You must not have heard me...."
4. "What do you mean, 'no'?...."
5. "Why...?"
6. "Who do you think you are, rejecting my idea so fast?"
7. "What the heck is wrong with you?"
....and if you are really honest about your thoughts....... "You dummy!"

The good news in all this is that, because change agents have experienced rejection before, they

C. 1996 S. Vineyard. STOP MANAGING VOLUNTEERS!

are careful how, when and who they approach in introducing change. (9-5)

Entrepreneurial leaders are constantly offering change as they work; it's in their blood. Because of past experiences and the fact that they are great observers of people around them, they consider change very, very carefully:

In planning changes, they:

1. Are clear about the goal.
2. Know who will be effected.
3. Know who will probably need to be recruited to help make it happen.
4. Know who will resist and how they might react.
5. Know how they plan to reward those who make it happen.
6. Estimate their gains and losses during and after the change happens.
7. Have weighed costs and mapped out responses; faced worst case scenarios.

In the first part of this chapter, I've looked at the change agent from an enlightened perspective; here however, I think it may be helpful to at least mention the darker side of having that role. Although not the norm, there are times when a change agent runs into real bear traps, set by people whose agenda is to stop your efforts. This goes well beyond the simple and normal resistance most people will have when a major change is announced. The bear trappers are in no mood to have their fears reduced or to listen to reason; theirs is a far different agenda, and thus I offer here a few survival tactics for your change-agent bag of tricks:

To sum it up: **Tread carefully:**

Watch out for expectations that are too high, and.......

Watch out for those people you might threaten.

Both can be bear traps that can stop you dead in your tracks or at the very least, make you lame enough to drain your energies.

When assessing a need for change, be sure that you can validate WHY the change is necessary. Be prepared to cite specific instances when the current response (or no response at all) to needs has been ineffective or detrimental. Have examples ready.

When designing something new, be sure you can document the expressed needs for what you propose, and why current systems or programs cannot meet those needs. Let me list some general reasons a new idea is needed :

No one else is meeting the need:

This becomes its own reason for creation.

Example: As people continue to be very mobile, traveling around the globe at record speed, stories began to abound of people becoming ill away from home and experiencing delays in treatment until information could be gathered about their personal medical history.

Change: Enter Medi-FAX, which offers, for an annual fee, the storing of all your medical history, drugs, treatments, allergies, etc. on computer.

Should an emergency arise, you would carry a card with your personal identification number (PIN#) which allows any medical treatment center or person to request an immediate FAX of those records to their site 24 hours a day!

Clearly, a need met with some entrepreneurial ingenuity and a visionary who designed a change that I would suspect many people will want to have as a safety precaution for themselves and their families. (Others, by the way, will NOT want any such service because they do not want their medical history in any location that they feel might be less than totally confidential....an assumption they might make about such a program. I interject this simply because even great ideas like this one do not appeal to everyone.)

If you have come up with a new idea that meets a need never before met, your chances for having it accepted are quite good.

Others are meeting the need: . BUT.....

This can be tricky and you must prove that even though others are addressing the need, you feel you can add something new because:

1. They are not meeting the need adequately; it's not enough or very good.
2. They are only meeting a small portion of the need; a few of the needy.
3. Their format, process, timing or location limit their ability to respond to the need.
4. Their effort is too slow.
5. Their effort is outdated; it does not meet current needs.

This kind of change, usually in the form of a program, is definitely in the "build a better mouse trap" category. That alone might make it seem as though you would get little or no resistance to your idea. Think again.

If you do not plan carefully, especially in assessing who might be upset by your effort, you might find that the very people you thought would welcome some "help" in addressing the need or those you had believed would be your closest allies because they led a parallel program, may be the very ones that set the bear-trap for you.

Watch for this especially when you are trying to change, update, augment or create any effort that might threaten what others feel is their "personal domain." Be assured that if they consider it a threat to what they feel is their "identity" or issymbolic to them, you may find bear traps all around you, though cleverly camouflaged.

I know whereof I speak and have the trap-marks to prove it. But I also have only myself to blame, because I didn't put enough caution into planning a project that included assessing who would be threatened by it and what tactics would be used to undermine the effort. In looking back and in having a lot of others relate their own horror stories of being blind-sided and shot-down when they least expected it, I've come up with some things you need to understand are weapons sometimes used to defeat a threatening idea or change:

☞ *Disinformation:* Information passed to others that is wrong and the passer knows it; it is usually given in an effort to recruit someone else to help in the fight against the change or idea. (Watch political opponents' ads on TV.... many take a quote out of context or quote a misrepresentation to marshal votes against the person.)

Targeted Disinformation: Same as previous but aimed at a pet project or specific interest of the targeted other; an attempt to put others in a panic that something they love & is significant to them is about to be destroyed if the change or effort comes about. (Watch for TV ads put out by the opposition of a bill before Congress to see such a tactic..... frequently geared toward panicking those most vulnerable.)

Personal Dis-crediting: Can't attack the idea so attacks the credibility, ethics, skills or motivation of the change agent; this can get very ugly and is often carried out through disinformation.

"Whispers-from-a-close friend": This one can hit you at two levels: personally and professionally. A person seen as "close" to you and therefore assumed to be "in the know", whispers to others that they are worried about what they know is really behind your effort, suggesting they know some "bad" stuff that they simply don't want to believe or divulge. That's a passive-aggressive masterpiece that is hard to track back, is quickly denied by the person if confronted and leaves blank spaces for listeners to fill in.They often do, then "pass it on", and its horrors grow with each re-telling.

In the hands of a very clever bear-trapper, it is the most powerful weapon imaginable: "trackless rumor-mongering" and elicits loud cries of "but I never meant to imply....." if you accuse the originator of using this to defeat your idea.

"If You Want My Support, Don't!": I once had a Pastor share his story of wanting to initiate some changes in a congregation ruled over by two wealthy, prominent and controlling families....founders of the church and pillars of the community. When he introduced the ideas, these wonderful people marched to the office of the Bishop and the home of various board members. Their message was the same: "If you support the Pastor, I will never support the church again and I will get others to withdraw their help too!"

It was a tough call for everyone involved and ended with the church splitting over the changes, the "pillars" taking their wallets and marching off to form a newcongregation. Those who stayed, welcomed the changes, found the funds to stand alone and two years later had not only stemmed the tide of departure that had been going on for years but also doubled their size and won back some who had followed the pillars!

Don't think, however that this is a "and they lived happily ever after" story. There was a blood-bath of gigantic proportions; some left the church in disgust at the conflict and never came back; the staff and Pastor were so exhausted they could hardly carry on their duties; good people were hurt and the Bishop tagged the Pastor's personnel file with a "trouble-maker" note that does not bode well for his future placements.

Whenever people draw the lines of "me or thee", it can be very nasty and almost no one will come out unscathed. Choose such battles carefully and check for weapons at the door.

I might guess that at this point in this book, you are either nodding in recognition of having lived through one of these tactics or, if you haven't, are thinking seriously of retreating to your bed and pulling the covers over your head.

Not all change agents encounter the negative situations shared here; most, in fact, plan their changes carefully enough to avoid such horror stories. Also, many changes are accepted and seen as the answer to specific needs, convincing people around you to cheer you on or at the very least, get out of your way.

To be effective as a leader of volunteer efforts, you will have to develop competencies in the area of change, with your most critical skills going into being a change agent . As you stretch toward continual improvement of procedures and processes, customer service and client responses, you will use change as a tool of choice and need to appreciate all of its facets and effects.

Keeping an eye out for the most camouflaged bear-traps, however, won't hurt.

Change

Change must be introduced carefully to realize its full potential. This worksheet can be of help in bringing change about positively.

What change do you propose? What is its goal?

What will it replace? Who might feel ownership of this older thing?

Who/what will be impacted by the change?

Who are the key stake-holders in this change?

How will each of these stake-holders feel about the change? What will/can their role be in the change?

Of those that may oppose the change, what are their objections? How can you address or remove these objections?

How will you assure people of what will happen to them in the change? How will you keep people informed as the change is planned and executed?

How will you reward people who positively help with the change?

How will you celebrate at the point the change is completed and bears fruit?

Organizational Change:
Leadership Tasks During Phases of Transition

Endings	Neutral Zone	New Beginnings
◆ Communicate what is/is not ending and why; avoid 'disengagement'	◆ Support people in not knowing for sure how they feel: don't force premature commitments	◆ Build sense of TEAM.
◆ Avoid sense of failure; use Nature metaphor: changing of the seasons is natural process of growth	◆ Avoid premature everything: decisions, structures, systems, etc. Set up Temporary Systems.	◆ Create/communicate Vision of future at organizational and personal levels
◆ Be clear, definite, open. Explain reasons for change - people must know 'why' in order to let go.	◆ Keep focus on progression; tolerate some regression; expect occasional chaos.	◆ Involve people in implementation of vision' practice 'Consensus Model' for development of new system.
◆ Inform people about the transition process and what personal impact change will have.	◆ Create or allow opportunities for reflection, withdrawal, retreat, etc. Allow people time to process feelings.	◆ Provide training in new reality/values/skills.
◆ Expect emotional reactions: denial, anger, depression, bargaining, resistance. The best response to these feelings is to support people in expressing them.	◆ Expect some disorientation, but don't let it become disintegration.	◆ Reward performance that leads to new vision.
◆ Expect people to highly value past patterns of behavior and systems which they didn't like much before.	◆ Plan for slump in productivity, programs.	◆ Provide rituals/symbols of the new beginning.
◆ Provide opportunities to grieve and say goodbye to the past: acknowledge feelings, provide rituals of separation, allow feeling of closure.	◆ People with a high need to structure will have an especially difficult time with this phase.	◆ Celebrate success.
◆ Honor the results and people of the past system.	◆ The most common error in the neutral zone is to make premature decisions: e.g., people who marry on the rebound.	◆ It will be very difficult to predict what a New Beginning will look like. Be open for new possibilities, new structures, new anything that might emerge. New ideas from others with indicate that they are beginning to accept Change.

c. 1996. Sue Vineyard. Stop Managing Volunteers.

Organizational Change:
Types of Loss During Organizational Transition

Types of Loss	Symptoms	Alleviators
1. **Attachment** Relationships Team Identity	Depression Sadness	Acknowledge Loss Ritualistic Endings
2. **Turf** Areas of Responsibility Influence	Rigidity Passivity Conflict	Negotiate New Responsibilities
3. **Structure** Patterns of Authority Policies, Deadlines Schedule	Out of Control	Develop New Temporary Structures
4. **Future** Promotions Opportunities Security	Demotivation Departures	Career Development Counseling Information
5. **Meaning** Belief in the Organization	Challenging Rumor Mill	Establish Credible Rationale Honesty, Openness Allow Feedback
6. **Control** Amount of Influence People Have on Their Life	Sabotage Slow-downs	Information Involvement In Planning

A Change Management Assessment Form

How to use this form: Certain "givens" must be in place if a major change effort is to succeed. This form is designed to help appraise those "givens" in your organization. There are no right or wrong answers, just honest responses that give you a picture of how change might be received.

Rank each question as <u>Not True</u>; <u>Somewhat True</u>; <u>Significantly True</u>; <u>True</u>:

1. When change efforts are initiated, people are given a very clear definition of how success will be measured.

2. We have experienced recent successes in implementing major changes.

3. We have spent time learning from any recent efforts at change that did not succeed.

4. The trust level in this organization is high, especially between management and employees.

5. When changes are announced there is open dialogue about the disruptions it may create and the difficulties we may need to address in order to make the change successful.

6. When people have problems in implementing changes they feel free to communicate about them and ask for help in solving them.

7. When changes are being implemented people who should care about the success of the changes continue to ask about them and show interest in them.

8. The people responsible for overseeing change implementation are skilled listeners.

9. Our teams are good at teamwork.

10. Our teams are skilled at surfacing and resolving conflict.

11. When difficulties or disruptions arise people are quick to address and fix them rather than being quick to blame others.

12. The goals and purposes and potential benefits of change efforts are clearly communicated to everyone in the organization.

13. Successful change efforts are acknowledged and celebrated.

14. People and teams who invest special effort and dedication in making a change successful are acknowledged, credited and awarded.

15. We take the time to thoroughly plan for changes.

16. The people responsible for overseeing change are skilled at building trusting relationships.

17. People who express negative feelings about change are listened to and their concerns are addressed rather than being accused of being negative.

18. People who deliberately work against the success of a change experience punishing consequences for their behavior.

c. 1996. Sue Vineyard. Stop Managing Volunteers.

19. The organization offers training to people in coping with change & managing stress.

20. People in this organization are excited and expectant about what the future holds.

21. People are encouraged to learn from their daily experience and to communicate to others what they are learning.

22. Suggestions and ideas for improvement of our organization are given serious attention.

23. People have been equipped with the communication and creative problem solving skills necessary for shaping how a change is implemented.

Score 0 for every "not true"; 2 for "somewhat true"; 3 for "significantly true", 5 for "true."

If your scores are 0-40, you might want to delay the change effort until some of the specific issues identified have been addressed. The effort is likely to fail.

40-70: Be cautious. there are significant issues present or absent that could damage your hope of successfully accomplishing the goals of the change.

70-100: Go for it. Your team or organization is ready to pull it off. Congratulations!

Used with permission of creator, Mike Murray.

Chapter Ten

The Art of Conflict Resolution & Negotiation

There are few skills the volunteer program administrator will have to have more highly developed than that of handling conflict and being able to negotiate positive agreements.

Let me tell you candidly that what I share here is almost totally a reflection of the wisdom and guidance of the one person that I believe knows more about this topic than anyone else in North America, Elaine Yarbrough, Ph.D.

I had the great good fortune to first hear Elaine teach a class in communication and conflict resolution at the University of Colorado in 1988 and then was wise enough to continue to turn to her for more learning through the years. I am blessed to share a close friendship with Elaine and can therefore tap her incredible wisdom and great good sense when faced with a conflict that stumps me. I urge you to look over the references at the end of this book to know how to get Dr. Yarbrough's books, audio and video tapes on this topic.

Some Basic Tenants Regarding Conflict

#1: **Conflict is neither good nor bad. It simply is.**

How we respond to conflict through our interpretations and reactions is what brands conflict positive or negative. If I find that a colleague and I have conflicting interests, I can respond in several ways with the most extreme being:

To arm myself for a knock-down, drag-out battle and vow to kill her off or die trying......

or.....

Believe that the conflict offers an opportunity to explore options to allow both sets of interests to be satisfied in a highly creative, negotiated settlement.

The first response is a negative FIGHT!, the second is a positive CHALLENGE.

Between these two are varying levels of responses that can be explored and negotiated. The more positive the reactions are of the conflicting parties, the more constructive the conflict will be, or to paraphrase a popular quote:

"Conflict is neither good nor bad but thinking makes it so."

2. **Conflict generates energy. The trick is to harness it for the good.**

I am always amazed when I encounter individuals or groups who expend mega-energy non-productively when faced with conflict. I wonder what they think they accomplish by spending their time and energy focused on what's wrong rather than directing this same energy to finding solutions.

Such negative focus becomes a black hole of energy when people get stuck:

      a. Blaming others.
      b. Trying to avoid being blamed.
      c. Rehashing old hurts.
      d. Putting others down.
      e. Score-keeping.
      f. Trying to inflict pain on the others.
      g. Hysterically trying to protect their turf.

When people in conflict situations spend even the smallest amount of energy on any of these, it is wasted and unavailable for the tough work of finding common ground and negotiating resolutions.

3. **The goal in conflict needs to be a resolution acceptable to those involved.**

Too often the goal of conflict becomes "I win-You lose" or, more dangerous yet, burying it.

Understand that if any party involved in a conflict "loses", no one wins. Only the goal of win-win brings on acceptable resolution. Even if you are talking about minor spats, if one person loses, energy will be drained from efforts as the "loser" finds a way to get back at the "winner" or becomes depressed because they feel they are a bad person.

Trying to ignore a conflict in the hope that it will go away is not only naive but dangerous. Avoidance typically drives a conflict underground, where it simmers and waits to explode to the surface at a later time to confound and confuse future interactions.

4. **To resolve conflicts, the real issues must be uncovered.**

If you are involved directly in a conflict, you will have to be clear about your own goals. If you are trying to help others resolve a conflict, you will need to help them clarify their own needs.

When goals are unclear or when they conflict ("I want to confront Sam, but I don't want him to be mad at me.") it is almost impossible to move toward settlement.

Too many times people fight over peripheral issues or symptoms rather than root causes. One assistant volunteer director asked for my help in getting her old office back at her hospital. Her boss, the volunteer director, had taken it from her saying the space was needed for a computer area and that she should simply put her files & computer on a rolling cart and "use whatever desk is available."

The assistant had worked up a list of reasons to justify getting her old office back and wanted to present her thoughts in person to the director. I affirmed that everything on her list was valid, but challenged her to see that office space was not the real issue; fear, respect and position were.

Had she and her boss only fought over space, the real conflict (the director's jealousy over her assistant's popularity with volunteers and her administrative skills) would never have been addressed. Once the assistant realized what the base issues really were, she was able to put her energies into more productive solutions of resolving the conflict. (She got her office back and used it positively as she began a successful job search elsewhere.)

It is critical to uncover real issues. You may have to do so by peeling back layers of screens that hide base concerns. To do so there must be an understanding of the difference between ISSUES and ACTIONS.

An issue (Dr. Yarbrough uses the term *interest*) is a desire, concern, goal, fear or need.

A response (Yarbrough uses the term *position*.) is a solution to a problem or concern; it's what you do or a stand you take.

A response is something you choose while an issue is the base reason that caused you to make that choice.

You provide volunteers with a list of unacceptable behaviors on their job. That's your response action. It was selected because your issue or interest is ethical behavior in regard to clients and co-workers.

When you understand peoples' issues, you can move on to appropriate responses or positions. Sadly, when people do not understand what the real issue is they can generate inappropriate responses (For examples of this, watch politicians!)

A word of caution: Never assume another's issue. Find out specifically.

5. **Conflict must have the goal of problem-solving rather than making everyone happy and bosom buddies!**

One very dangerous impediment people in our field have to healthy conflict resolution is that they often want everyone to be happy and like everyone else.

To such people, conflict is not resolved until all parties hug and make up. If volunteer leaders are to rise to a new level of competency, they will need to leave such goals behind.

Not everyone is going to like and be friends with everyone else. Workers can co-exist in a parallel fashion, successfully interacting on common goals without being great friends or agreeing on every issue outside their commonality. One person can respect another's expertise without liking them personally or agreeing on being a vegetarian!

Keep in mind in working with others that "if it doesn't matter—don't let it matter." I'm not crazy about men wearing their hair to their waist, but that does not matter if such a person and I have the assignment to work together to pack boxes of food for distribution to the poor.

Also let go of the belief that for you to personally be successful in resolving conflicts, everyone must come out liking you. If that sounds too difficult for you to accept, keep in mind that people around you need you to be *effective* more than they need you to be *nice.* Stay focused on the problems to be solved and do not stray into side issues that can actually inhibit effective conflict resolution.

Reaching Agreements; Negotiating for Positive Results

To reach good agreements, Dr. Yarbrough tells us that we must focus on three areas:

> #1. Creating common grounds.
> #2. Loosening deadlocks.
> #3. Creating specific expectations & consequences.

Creating Common Grounds:

Whether you are trying to negotiate a resolution of conflict or starting to work on a project with other groups, begin with what you have in common. No matter how divergent the positions, different the backgrounds or hostile the parties, if you search widely enough, you'll find commonalties.

After establishing this common background, reach further to find a common vision. For example, a homeless shelter and a museum both have been in a community for 20+ years, seek to serve the population, tap volunteers and care about their city. That is part of their commonalties to date.

They each want to serve citizens more effectively, make their city a better place to live, uplift spirits and enlighten clients. That's their shared vision of the future.

Their conflict comes as the shelter plans to move next door to the museum and the latter is fearful that homeless people will spend most of their days loitering on their property and frightening volunteers and patrons away.

Loosening Deadlocks:

When people seem at opposite ends of a conflict, you will need to find a widening area of agreement by breaking deadlocks and negotiating positive results. Here are several strategies:

> #1: **Expanding the win-win area:** Go back to the steps mentioned in the chapter on Friend-raising and use them. What do you have to offer that might be of value to the others? What direct benefits might the opposition get if they help you attain your goal? Find out what people need and explore ways that you can meet those needs.

> #2: **Cut other's costs**: Figure out what is behind the resistance of others. What do they believe their cooperation will cost? Look at costs of time, energy, dollars, reputation, image, relationships, prestige, etc. Look for ways to reduce or eliminate such costs.

#3: Compensating: In exchange for cooperation, how could you reward the opposing party? Consider recognition, acclaim, direct assistance, greater support of a pet effort of theirs, etc.

#4: Small concessions: As you explore real issues, shared vision and compensation, any tensions that existed may be relaxed to the point that the parties may concede some smaller points. The museum leadership that is fighting about the shelter may concede, for example, that people who have nowhere to go have a right to shelter and that just because someone has no home does not mean that they can't respect the museum or appreciate art.
The shelter might concede that if multiple clients were permitted to linger all day on the museum front lawn, it could be disturbing to visitors.

#5: Bridging: Finding a middle ground that could satisfy a common vision and create a new option for resolution.
The museum could train several mission volunteers or clients to monitor their facility and prevent problems as well as welcoming museum visitors.

#6: Making small steps: Sometimes a conflict is too complex or vast to be solved all at once. It may also be that a real issue is trust between parties. Taking small steps toward resolution can help at such times. Having museum leaders invited to the mission's next board meeting and vice-versa might be a small first step.

#7: Setting objective criteria: If negotiation stalemates exist or people get stuck in a fierce win-lose position, you may need to step back and regroup thinking by setting acceptable criteria........
"Neither the museum nor the mission leadership will make decisions regarding things of common impact without consulting the other."

....or....

"We will meet one week from today, each bringing three people who have volunteered to form a joint resolution committee."

#8: Compromising: This is a "lets split the difference" solution where no one gets all they wanted. Don't jump to this too quickly, however. Dr. Yarbrough offered the classic example of this from the story of two people fighting over an orange. They compromised too quickly by cutting the orange in half and never discovered that one wanted to eat the pulp, the other only wanted the rind for grating. Had they explored real issues they could have each gotten their needs met!

Getting Specific: A Measurable Agreement

When you have negotiated a resolution it is time to be specific on what has been agreed to AND what the consequences will be if the agreement is broken. You may even want to be specific about any fine-tuning or adjustments that are needed later and how these will be negotiated.

Avoid fluff statements in your agreements that almost guarantee future conflict. "Being neighborly" or "getting along" are open to interpretation and really say nothing concrete. Keep in mind that a better word for communication is *interpretation* and try to eliminate statements that must be left to interpretation.

Be specific about who does what, when, where and how. Attach times, dates, etc. List ultimate goals you have set and find ways to make them measurable. Draw up lines of authority and responsibility so that everyone knows who to turn to to answer questions that arise. Spell out any joint property or financial issues most carefully.

Decide at the beginning what the consequences will be if the agreement is broken and how infractions will be handled and judged. Set times to check on progress and discuss ways to openly recognize and reward those people who help make the agreement work.

Gosh, you might even plan a celebration of the successful negotiation!

Conflict resolution and negotiation are a natural part of the job of volunteer program leaders. Knowing how to identify commonalties, uncover real issues, trade value for value, generate acceptable solutions and plan specifically for actions will help everyone be more effective.(10-1)

And that, after all, is the bottom line.

Conflict

Areas of conflict that exist in your program:

How people have handled these conflicts in the past; what resulted? (Consider all responses- even ignoring a conflict is a response.)

What are real issues behind each conflict?

What are goals/needs of the people conflicting?

What resolutions would satisfy needs of those conflicting?

What deadlocks exist? How might they be loosened?

What specific agreements need to be documented?

Chapter Eleven

Dealing With Problematic Volunteers

Hang on. This section speaks of the unspeakable:

Volunteers that cause real trouble.
Turkeys. Spoiled brats. Meanies.

In our general society, issues that were previously taboo to talk about have come out of the closets and even become topics for the media to explore, and often exploit......

—-Incest. Extreme self-serving behavior. Abuse. Corruption. Brutality. Ineptitude.

All manner of dysfunctional behavior.

Although not as sensational, volunteerism has had its own closet topic that some people would rather I'd avoid talking about because it seems too harsh to be part of our image of effective, caring concern for others. The "be-nice" school of thinking.

My response to such critics of reality and open discussion is simple:

> *If we want to be as effective as possible and really care about others we will*
> *stop pretending that we never have to deal with some very difficult volunteers.*

Not the volunteer that is slightly annoying or needy, somewhat bothersome and misdirected, but really problematic volunteers who eat up your time and drain energy from everyone and everything..

> ....People who demand control and have been around so long and brought their
> friends, relatives and other like-minded dysfunctionals into a program that
> the term incestuous becomes appropriate.

> ....Volunteers who are abusive, verbally, emotionally and even physically with
> clients, staff and other volunteers.

.... Volunteers who are corrupt and unethical—betraying confidences, using resources inappropriately and snooping in client files.

.... Volunteers who are brutal, bullying others with their power; who threaten to withdraw support if not pleased. Those who use their influence to blackmail in order to get their way or hold people hostage with threats and promises.

.... Volunteers who are inept yet "untouchable" because some authority dictates their role in a program. Placed in positions for which they have no background, refusing to learn necessary skills because their interest lies only in the prominence the position affords them.

.... Self-serving and spoiled volunteers whose behavior has not been checked for one poor reason or another.

Like popular talk shows of the 90's, these problematic volunteers lurk in our closets, displaying all manner of dysfunctional behaviors.

Arrogant. Spoiled. Nasty. Hidden-agenda. Unbalanced. Bigoted. Dangerous.

Their toll is great and is typically greatest as they, who are in the vast minority, take up the vast majority of a leader's time and energy. One volunteer director in a care facility that I worked with determined that the five volunteers causing real trouble out of her corps of 122, actually took up 65% of her time and energy!

Every program has them at one time or another.

Lets look at some myths in regard to these very troublesome volunteers. This list and the worksheets at the end of this segment, may help you clarify the depth of problems you face because of difficult volunteers. If you find yourself believing one of the following, you may have to readjust your thinking as you plan your strategy in dealing with identified problems.

The MYTH statements that confound problems & make them worse......

1. Ignoring a problem will make it go away.

WRONG. It may go underground and be more difficult to confront, but it will not go away, unless, of course, you plan to simply wait for the person to die, the height of avoidance.

2. No one else notices. I'm the only one who is suffering.

You must be kidding. Others see the problem and can shift their anger or frustration to you, wondering why you don't take control and stop the negative behavior.

3. I can fix/change the problem person.

WRONG. You can't and shouldn't. That's not why you're there. "Fixing" volunteers will drain your energy, time and effectiveness and ignore the 98% of volunteers who are doing a great job. Keep in mind, I am not talking about people who are causing minor problems and simply need to be set straight....I'm talking about real trouble-makers who are dysfunctional.

C. 1996 S. Vineyard. STOP MANAGING VOLUNTEERS!

4. There's good in everyone. I just need to give them time to show it.

WRONG. There are some nasty people. How they got that way is not your problem or challenge. Savior is not in your job description. Time won't fix everyone and in the meantime you'll lose good people and possibly hurt some clients who don't deserve to put up with abuse.

5. If I confront them, it will make things worse.

Not if you do it carefully and calmly. NOT confronting problematic behavior will cause more trouble, however.

6. If I confront them they'll leave and the program will die.

If your program rides on the whim of one individual, you need to look for a new job. That is simply too much control, power and dependence for one person.

7. If I'm really the caring and all-accepting person I should be, I can handle them.

STOP IT! You are beginning to believe your own press clippings. You're a volunteer administrator, not a saint. Don't see other people's dysfunction as somehow a test of your worth. They are the problem, not you.

8. If I push them out they will be mad at me.

Maybe. Maybe not. If they become angry, so be it. You did what was best for the program and the people it serves. Sticks and stones and all of that....

Others may actually be relieved to be out of a situation that was uncomfortable for them.

All of the above are MYTHS. They are WRONG. Eight times wrong. (Well maybe only 7 1/2 times wrong.) (11-1)

Some Hard Truths

In addition to the myth statements just listed, let's also look at some hard truths. This is where we separate the volunteer program leaders who can accept tough love and those who think such statements have "no place in true volunteering." How you look at these next few paragraphs will probably be in direct proportion to your effectiveness of ridding your program of problematic volunteers.

Hard truth #1:

Volunteers are NOT your clients.

Many people who lead volunteer programs have, usually unconsciously, confused the difference between a client and a volunteer. They believe that because a great part of their job is to nurture and support volunteers that they are therefore responsible for them as individuals.

Not so.

As a volunteer program leader you are responsible for the actions of all your workers....
volunteer, paid, stipend, assigned or post-service rewarded.

You work to support, direct and control those actions, aiming them toward specific goals and the general mission of your organization.

When workers... paid or non-paid... spend their energies negatively and cause trouble that results in impeding progress, harming others or otherwise keeping you from attaining goals in the most effective manner, you must be ready to exert control and STOP the negative behavior.

What you would not tolerate in a paid staff person you should not tolerate in a non-paid or stipend staff volunteer.

You cannot step in and stop poor behavior, however, if you see a volunteer as some form of client for whom you are responsible. Such thinking can expand to your believing that you are obligated to accept the volunteer no matter what their behavior and can also prevent you from seeing volunteers as part of your staff.

Except in specific programs where those receiving services are put to work as part of their therapy, volunteers are not clients. They are part of the corps of workers serving clients and are there first and foremost to serve, not be served.

Hard Truth #2:

Not everyone with problems can or wants to be "fixed."

Put away your fix-it kit. Some people cannot be fixed, at least not by you.

Even if you have the skills to help some dysfunctional volunteer, you do not have the time, energy or job assignment for the task.

Also, keep in mind that some people enjoy being dysfunctional at a certain level.

That obnoxious person who is crude and rude loves the attention it brings her. She jolts your sensibilities and you can't ignore her, no matter how much you try. The result of your trying to "put up" with this abrasive bully or trying to appease her in the hope that she will mellow out only feeds her dysfunctional goal which is, "By God, you won't dismiss me Bub! You'll pay attention to me if I have to kill myself to get you to notice me."

The dependent person who constantly wants someone to listen to her latest story of victimization loves it when she is consoled, defended and offered sympathy. She's won her game of "Poor me/Save me" and those who intervene to solve her problems only fuel her dysfunction of refusing to take control of her own life.

Hard Truth #3:

You can't accept everyone who wants to work with your program.

You are not responsible for the fact that some people who come to volunteer in your agency are NOT really a good match.

Inclusiveness is a philosophy, not a mandate.

          C. 1996 S. Vineyard. STOP MANAGING VOLUNTEERS!

Some examples are obvious: The drug abuser is not a good match in a hospital setting; the child molester should not be a school crossing guard.

More subtle examples may be less obvious:

> ...A hyper or over-reactive person is not a wise choice for a crisis line.

> ...A gossip should not have access to confidential files.

> ...A bigot should not help clients fill out service application forms.

> ...An insensitive, verbal bully should not work with abused elderly.

> ...A chronic complainer should not deal with the press.

> ...A back-stabber should not be a team leader.

Accepting everyone who knocks at your door is trouble in the making. Yes Virginia, there is a Santa Claus, but not every Santa is a jolly old soul.

Hard Truth #4:

Some adults act like spoiled children.

They believe they own the program. It is "theirs" and no one, especially yourself, should mess with it. Never. Ever.

Such people pout, threaten, try to gather others to fight any change and can become quite viscous if they are not "obeyed."

They can easily lose sight of the goal of serving clients and substitute it with their own needs of retaining their position, control, celebrity or image.

What they do revolves around what they see as best for them rather than the program. They employ martyrdom and "after all I've done..." statements as they try cohering others to "be on their side."

They throw sophisticated and often dangerous temper tantrums that deal with score-keeping, threats of non-support and long litanies of justification for killing new ideas they feel threaten them. They have a turf they see as their divine right and can turn on anyone that moves toward it. They are good at masking attacks with platitudes, sweet talk and statements that begin: "I hate to say anything, but...." They use disinformation and misinformation to fuel games of "let's have you and them fight." Divide and conquer strategies abound.

Spoiled adults are problematic in their mildest forms and deadly in their most intense. Since spanking is unacceptable, you will have to find other ways to deal with them.

Hard Truth #5:

It can be hard to mix established volunteers with new age volunteers.

Newer, more diverse volunteers sometimes can be seen as visitors from outer space by the existing, more traditional volunteers. It can be a real challenge to negotiate new rules of behavior for Baby Boomers, for example, that are acceptable to the older, more experienced volunteers who have many years of involvement and are used to certain patterns of behavior from other workers.

My 87 year old aunt in Wilmington, DE is a real exception to the norm because she just "loves to have the younger folks come to volunteer at the church...they bring new, fresh ideas and look at things so differently from those of us old fogies who have been around since Martha Washington's time!"

More typically, long-term volunteers comfortable with their patterns of helping and established routines balk at job-sharing, episodic volunteers, flex-space and flex-time. It is the wise volunteer leader who sees their criticism and discomfort as stemming from uncertainty over change rather than a fatal attack of nastiness.

Ways to Confront and Gain Control

When, for any reason, volunteers cause unacceptable problems, there are three steps I suggest you try to correct the action:

#1: Talk with them in private; document the effects their actions have had. Remind them of their commitment to the clients served and how more appropriate actions are required to better serve these people. Ask why they chose this action and if there are any extenuating circumstances of which you are not aware.

Listen to their responses carefully, correcting any improper assumptions or understandings; do not project acceptance of their behavior, but explain why it was inappropriate. Don't get into a debate over issues that are not debatable. Avoid side issues; focus on the problem.

Set a way to measure new behavior; establish a time in which the behavior will be corrected and a time for the two of you to meet again to measure progress and results. Focus on the issues, never the personality; avoid negative-you messages. End with a projection of your confidence that they can change the behavior.

#2: At the second meeting, review the actions that have taken place since the first interview. Document any continued problems and efforts. Set a very short time frame in which the person must correct any inappropriate behavior and outline consequences if the actions are not remedied. Follow this meeting up with a letter outlining progress along with their assurance that the behavior will change before your next scheduled meeting; outline consequences. Put this letter in their personnel file.

#3: If by the third meeting the behavior is not corrected, produce the document created in #2 above, reviewing the agreement and consequences of non-compliance. Follow through on the consequences, typically either removal to a different work site or total removal from the program. Document your discussion and place it in your file.

All of this probably sounds far too stringent to many of you; to others it sounds exactly right.

Frankly I hope you never have to tap into such hard-edged process, and I would expect that few of you would. Most people, who have acted inappropriately, will correct the problems immediately after having it pointed out to them. Sometimes they are simply looking for a way to have their concerns heard, and a quiet discussion with you may satisfy this need for attention.

If however, this is not the case, it is up to the volunteer administrator to step in and prevent the clients or program from being damaged. It's not easy, but it is necessary.

Problematic volunteers exist. We cannot pretend they do not. Horror stories abound and I am sure you can offer some of the best. (11-2)

The effective volunteer program leader must come to grips with the reality of such volunteers and the problems they leave in their wake. They must be prepared to deal with them fairly, openly and swiftly and have sound, documented reasons for removing any from a program.

As difficult as it is to "fire" a volunteer, it is more difficult in the long run to hide from the confrontation that will either remedy the negative behavior or remove it from contaminating everything you and the overwhelming number of wonderful volunteer and paid staff are trying to accomplish.

There will always be turkeys, but they don't have to gobble in your arena.

Problematic Volunteers

Assumptions that inhibit solutions that Problematic Volunteers create:
Example: You can't "fire" a volunteer.

Problem Analysis

Specific problems caused by volunteers: Example: not keeping required records of actions.

Specific difficulties their actions caused: Example: No way to tell authorities what was done; can't put in budget, etc.

How volunteer will be confronted; by whom; when:

What volunteer offered as to why they acted; responses designed to remediate incorrect action:

Chapter Twelve

The Healthy Climate

Throughout this book, I have referred to the organizational climate of any agency or program. We looked at it in greatest depth as we explored creativity, then touched on it in other sections in regard to friend-raising, change, Leadershift, etc.

Climate deserves such multi-faceted attention, because it deals with feelings....how it feels to a volunteer, paid staff person, funder or client. How it feels as people work together; as they assess success or failure; as the public perceives the work, etc.

Experience has taught us that any agency can have perfect by-laws, rules of procedures, policies and organizational charts and look wonderful on paper, BUT, if it doesn't "feel" right to the people who must interact there, this perfectly-crafted program can fall apart.

Feelings are facts to those who experience them. They are also difficult to explain, elusive, ever-changing and different for different people.

All of these factors make it imperative that the volunteer program administrator, the "ultimate leader" we looked at in previous chapters, rises to new levels of competency in understanding, formulating and maintaining a healthy climate. You may find this impossible to do in your larger organization, but you do have more control of the climate to a great degree within your own volunteer program.

As you look over the worksheets throughout this book, you will recognize that many of them have to do with the feel of the climate. Many are tools to help you uncover what is going on beneath the work-surface of your program; they are designed to get to root problems, community values, worker attitudes, etc. which are part of the climate that exists around specific competencies of creativity, change, etc..

Here I want you to take a step back and look at climate as a whole; to the general feel of your workplace, so that you have the tools to assess, encourage or remediate any parts that may need your attention.

A Review of Components

For a quick review, keep in mind that organizational climate is made up of four dimensions: Energy, Distribution of Energy, Growth and Pleasure.

These dimensions come to life through the unwritten rules that govern behavior, which are called Norms. Some of these norms become so strong that they are actually written down in policy statements; these are labeled Super Norms.

How norms are enforced in your organization has a lot to do with how it feels in your workplace.

Let's look at these components more closely as they relate to your entire program or organization. Assessment worksheets you find at the end of this chapter will help you do this in greater depth.

Energy:

Every gathering of people has an inherent energy. Meetings, conferences, programs, projects, groups, etc. all have an energy level that you can sense with very little observation. Typically, those groups of people who feel imminent threat, those just beginning an effort, those trying out new ideas, those feeling they have a say in what they do, or those whose members believe they are righting a wrong will have high energy.

Conversely, those groups of people who are doing the same old thing by rote, are depressed because they are not appreciated, are fearful about reprimands, feel they have no control over their actions, cannot see how their work "fits" with the greater goal of the organization, and those feeling that what they do is fruitless will have low energy.

The difference is stimulation versus de-motivation. The people themselves probably have about the same energy to offer, but with the latter, de-motivated group, much of their energy is going into having to survive, being confused, or depressed. When we drain off energy negatively, we cannot get it back. Look closely at your people for any energy drains they might be dealing with as a whole. When looking at individuals, note energy drains that are coming from the other segments of their life and effecting their work. (12-1)

Distribution of Energy:

Where people put the energy they bring to their work is critical for you to understand.
You want to make sure that it is put into productive efforts and not wasted on those matters which are non-productive, or, worse yet, counter-productive. Let me begin a list for you that might assist you in assessing where energy is "spent" in your program and how to label it. Your own list will be much more helpful for you, as it will look at your own specific program characteristics.

Energy for	Productive Use	Non-Productive	Counter-Productive
Specific work	Do it well	Avoid it	Do it incorrectly
Relationships	Healthy, open	Closed, fearful	Accusatory, wound
Spokesperson	Good info to good people; tells story	Never mentions	Negative focus, lies

Attitude	Positive, forgives, believes in vision, problem-solves.	Stuck on negatives & problems, whines.	Riles others; negative & blocking positives.
Planning	Sees ahead, keeps vision in mind, leads way, encourages others, can do!	Stuck on non-issues; obscures vision; whines.	Blocks vision; naysayer wants own way; threatens.

As you draw up your own list, you will want to concentrate on taking it the next step by asking yourself: (12-2)

#1:   How can I reinforce the productive use of energy?

#2:   How can I redirect non-productive use of energy toward more productive?

#3:   How can I eliminate counter-productive drain of energy, and if I can't, how do I get rid of those who use their energy this way?

Understanding climate is not an exercise in knowledge for knowledge's sake, but a tool to use for pro-active response to that knowledge and an understanding of what to DO with the information you observe.

When you see positive energy being used in productive ways, you will want to look deeper at it and figure out what shaped it that way. What norms are part of this good use of energy? What made people so productive? What feeds them as they work so that they continue to be productive?

You may wish to call together a small task force to discuss your climate and literally list those factors you all believe go into this positive facet of your climate. My guess is you would find many of the factors below and add many more of your own:

 The positive attitude of leaders.
Open communication.
Good training and preparation for work.
Healthy staff-volunteer relationships.
Direct supervision by staff overseeing work.
A clear vision of the end goal.
An understanding of the mission of the organization.
Appropriate and timely recognition.
Fun.
Flexibility.
Permission to create and suggest.
A lack of fences or forbidden territory people need access to.
No prima-donnas.
Appreciation for diversity.
Focus on commonalties.
Willingness to listen to new ideas & a commitment to change if they work better.
A balance between authority and responsibility.
A say in what happens to people or their work.
An understanding that people have a life outside this work.
Acceptance of differences.

An interesting variety of work.
Appropriate placement.
A sense of teamwork or family.
A good healthy dose of common sense in decision-making.
Processes that stimulate rather than stymie; they make sense.
Encouragement and cheer leading by others.
Skill-building.

The list could go on, and will, as you identify those factors that go into creating and encouraging a continuing productive use of energy.

Growth & Pleasure:

When people feel they have grown because of what they have accomplished, they feel good about it. They also get good feelings from seeing measurable growth in accomplishing the greater goal of the organization. Can you even imagine how great paid staff and volunteers felt after years of raising money for research on polio when Dr. Jonas Salk developed his successful vaccine for that awful disease?

Everyone of them, along with every person who ever donated a dime to that cause, had reason to celebrate! What they did grew into success, and they were a part of the growth. How wonderful!

At a personal level, people can look back and realize how much they have grown in their affiliation with a job or assignment. The shy person who can now speak before an audience because she had to recruit volunteers from local service clubs can see her growth.

A young person who was unsure of himself before having to enlist sponsors for a walkathon, but now does so in ever-widening circles, can see his growth (and so can his family) and feel a sense of pride as well as transferring his new-found confidence to other areas of his life.

These examples demonstrate growth factors that can be measured. Sometimes you, as the leader of your program, will need to point out the growth to individuals or groups who have gotten bogged down in the daily assignments and overlooked the bigger picture that shows growth.

Find creative ways to remind people of growth. The United Way does this very effectively through its community display of a thermometer that shows it moving up toward its financial goal. Why not try a contest among staff and volunteers of a symbol that would be equally as effective and demonstrate how your program is moving toward its goal. It may take a bit of creativity but my bet is on someone coming up with some way to measure growth!

Being able to see growth is part of the fourth dimension of climate: Pleasure. It pleases people to see success and have others acknowledge it. It may be more tricky to measure pleasure in people and groups, but it can be done.

This is the real "feeling" base of organizational climate. Pleasure is a feeling. It is user-oriented and unique to different people. It is expressed differently by different people, and in some cases, felt but not expressed by other, more reticent, people.

Let me list some aspects of climates that I have observed were present when people expressed and demonstrated pleasure. Please draw up a list for your own program.

➡️ A lot of the things I listed under distribution of energy. You choose.

Trust...of one another, the parent agency, the mission & ethics of the leaders.

Laughter.

Personalized work spaces with pictures, stuffed animals, plants, etc.

Obvious respect among all workers; no cliques or label-groups.

Appropriate affection & caring among workers.

Thoughtfulness.

Celebrations of birthdays, holidays, special occasions, etc.

Willingness to help one another, even if outside job descriptions.

Maturity.

Focus on the mission; getting work done effectively.

Willingness to admit errors, say "I'm sorry" and move on.

A lack of gunny-sacking past grievances.

No hint of bigotry or "ism"s of any nature.

No bullies allowed to try their trickery.

No hidden agenda or buried conflict; good conflict resolution.

Involvement outside the worksite, but no pressure for all to join in.

Acceptance of differences, especially differently-abled people.

A whole lot of balloons!

I add this last item as a serious part of climates I have observed that participants would describe as highly pleasurable because I was always struck by the fact that they all had balloons tucked somewhere....even ones that had lost their air or helium and were tacked to bulletin boards, taped on work stations or carefully spread under a desk's glass top! It was an incredible symbol of healthy programs I came to look for in my work as "Organizational Doctor." (12-3)

> One Last note on healthy dimensions of a climate: It seems to me that there is a need for another chapter on wellness of people, because how emotionally healthy people are determines a great deal of the wellness of the climate in which they reside. Such a chapter will have to wait for another book and time. I examined personal wellness in my 1989 book, "How to Take Care of You, So You Can Take Care of Others' and I would refer you to it if you want more on this topic.
>
> You also need to know that another book swirling around in the back of my brain looks specifically at wellness from the organizational and personal perspectives simultaneously. I hope to have it out in the next two years because I believe it is critical to the future success of all our programs. Until then, be well.

Norms

All of the above dimensions have unwritten rules to tell people how to behave. Your own organization and program have dozens, if not hundreds, of them swirling around and identifying them can be very helpful in diagnosing the wellness level of your climate.

How those norms are enforced is also critical, as it sets an attitude of fear or support throughout your ranks.

When norms are broken, do the people in your program punish the offender negatively or work to correct them? If a newcomer arrives late on the job does someone jump all over him in front of others, chastise and threaten him and embarrass his socks off? Or does his supervisor take him away to a private area and share with him how important it is to be punctual and how much pride everyone takes in being on time?

The first choice is punitive, the second is informative, fair, and sensitive but direct.

As you examine norms in your program, look carefully at how they are enforced. Many good efforts have had appropriate norms surrounding their work but have had inappropriate enforcement and have suffered because of it. (12-4; 12-5)

One tip: Never put the norm-enforcement responsibility in the hands of someone who is arrogant, up-tight about "everyone must obey the rules to the letter!" or has a cherished picture of Atilla the Hun over their desk. You may have to root out such people and talk to them about appropriate ways to coach people and easing up on dotting every i and crossing every t. Inflexible people rarely make good enforcers.

In all of this, you are talking about wellness. We have had too many examples of workers going berserk in postal offices, universities, government facilities, manufacturing plants and restaurants and shooting others over pent-up grievances, Many of those horror stories come out of a poor climate, and although the vast majority of responsibility for those destructive acts must rest with the crazed person who carried them out, they serve as a wake-up call for all of us to recognize the impact the feel of the workplace has on all of us.

If we are to increase our competencies to meet the challenges we face today and into the new century in volunteerism, we must make ourselves aware of the subtleties of the feelings, attitudes and unspoken messages of our workplaces.

As even these change and shift from in-house to community placements, we must find ways to measure what we have, select what we want to continually support, identify what must be eliminated and stimulate new responses so that people can be empowered to do the work.

In our fast-paced, go-go, drive-through lifestyles, time and energy are the new currencies. It is up to the leaders who direct volunteer energies to see to it that people who become involved can invest and spend each with maximum effectiveness, enabled by a climate of trust, encouragement, empowerment and vision.

This challenge will take all the competencies we can master in order to lead volunteer energies toward the meeting of growing needs in our communities. As times evolve, new competencies we cannot even imagine today, will be necessary for our survival and effectiveness.

It is no longer enough to simply know how to manage volunteers directly or recite the principles of planning, organizing, staffing, directly and evaluating their work. Our challenges are much wider, deeper and more complex. They are at once more tangible and more subtle, more gray and more black & white. They depend on information and interpretation, more "know the boundaries" and more "boundaryless".

Our job descriptions cannot begin to lay out all of the paradoxes we face today or in the future. Just when we find answers to problems, the problems will change. We must be armed with competencies in Leadershift, management, change, creativity, recognition, conflict resolution, handling difficult people, entrepreneurial thinking, reshaping our organizations, broadening our resource base, working with staff and organizational climate.

We must stop managing volunteers exclusively without ever forgetting HOW to manage the incredible energies and resources they bring us, and work through others to best harness and direct those energies and resources.

And through it all we must never forget the "why" of our purpose; the vision of what **can** be against the reality of what is.

Volunteerism is an energy force equal to any task brought before it. It is rich and alive and all-powerful.

As long as we have faith in that basic, simple conviction, we will find within ourselves the strength to grow, in our competencies and our convictions, to make miracles happen.

Energy

What kind of energy level exists in your program for the following categories? What prompts this energy level? Note any energy drains.

Paid Staff:

Volunteers:

Clients:

Governing Board & Administration:

Distribution of Energy

Where is energy used in your program? "Grade" each use as productive, non-productive or counter-productive.

How might you reinforce the positive uses of energy and reduce or eliminate that which is non- or counter-productive?

Growth & Pleasure

What opportunities for growth exist for both paid and volunteer staff?

How can more growth opportunities be build into your program?

What do volunteers find pleasurable while working with your program?

What additional things might be introduced to increase pleasure?

Norms

List the norms (unwritten rules that govern behavior) that exist in your program with the four dimensions of organizational climate:

Energy:

Distribution of Energy:

Pleasure:

Growth:

How are norms enforced? How do new people learn about your norms?

12-4

Categories of Norms

When examining norms, you will typically find them in the categories that follow. Identifying the rules that tell people how to behave helps you diagnose strengths & weaknesses. Categories include:

1. Organizational demands: rules, structures, red tape, etc.

2. Supervision: honest delegation? responsibility, empowerment, etc.

3. Rewards: fairness, appropriateness, positive or negative, creative? etc.

4. Warmth/support: helpfulness? expressed appreciation & support? etc.

5. Conflict: is questioning OK? is conflict handled positively?

6. Physical setting: does it empower & enable? is it fun? personalized? etc.

7. Identity: do people feel connected? that they belong & are valued team members? etc.

8. Standards: are group values high? is honesty prized? etc.

9. Creativity/risk: is creativity encouraged? rewarded? can people challenge others? etc.

Bibliography

A list of useful books on topics referred to in the teaching text:

Bryson, John & Crosby, Barbara. **Leadership for the Common Good.** Jossey-Bass. San Francisco, Ca.

Burke, Mary Ann & Liljenstolpe, Carl. **Creative Fund Raising.** Crisp Books. Menlo Park, CA.

Covey, Stephen. **Principle-Centered Leadership.** Summit Books. New York, NY.

Drucker Foundation. **Self Assessment Tool for Nonprofit Organizations.** Points of Light Foundation, Volunteer Readership catalog. Washington, DC.

Drucker, Peter. **Post Capitalist Society; The New Realities.** Harper Collins Publishers, New York, NY.

Ellis, Susan. **From the Top Down.** Energize Books, Philadelphia, PA.

Gabor, Andrea. **The Man Who Discovered Quality.** Penquin Books. New York, NY.

Iacocca, Lee. **Iacocca.** Bantam Books. New York, NY.

Kennedy, Allen & Deal, Terrence. **Corporate Cultures.** Addison-Wesley Publishing. Reading, MA.

Kennedy, Larry. **Quality Management in the Nonprofit World.** Jossey-Bass. San Francisco, CA.

Kindler, Herbert. **Managing Disagreement Constructively.** Crisp Books. Menlo Park, CA.

Kouzes, James & Posner, Barry. **The Leadership Challenge.** Jossey-Bass. San Francisco, CA.

Lynch, Richard. **Lead!** Jossey-Bass. San Francisco, CA.

McCurley, Steve. **Volunteer Management: Mobilizing All The Resources In Your Community; Volunteer Management Policies; Recruiting Volunteers for Difficult Assignments.** all from: Heritage Arts Publishing, 1807 Prairie Ave., Downers Grove, IL. 60515. orders: 1-800-272-8306.

Minnesota Office of Volunteer Services. **Planning It Safe.** MOVS. St. Paul, MN.

Moore, Gail & Mackenzie, Marilyn. **Building Credibility With The Powers That Be.** Partners Plus. Don Mills, Ontario, Canada.

Naisbitt, John & Aburdene, Patricia. **Megatrends 2000; Megatrends for Women.** Villard Books, New York, NY.

Points of Light Foundation. **No Surprises!** Washington, DC.

Rifkin, Jeremy. **The End of Work.** Tarcher/Putnam Books, New York, NY.

Seita, Trudy & Waechter, Sue. **Change.** Heritage Arts Publishing, 1807 Prairie Ave., Downers Grove, IL. 60515. orders: 1-800-272-8306.

Temme, James. **Total Quality Customer Service.** Temme & Associates. Scottsdale, AZ.

Vineyard, Sue. **Beyond Banquets, Plaques & Pins; The Great Trainer's Guide; Evaluating Volunteers, Programs & Events; 101 Ideas for Volunteer Programs; 101 Tips for Volunteer Recruiting; 101 MORE Ideas for Volunteer Programs; 101 Ways to Raise Resources; Managing Volunteer Diversity; How to Take Care of You; Secrets of Motivation; Secrets of Leadership; Marketing Magic for Volunteer Programs; Megatrends & Volunteerism; GRAPEVINE: Volunteerism's Newsletter.** Heritage Arts Publishing, 1807 Prairie Ave., Downers Grove, IL. 60515. orders: 1-800-272-8306.

Wellins, Richard & Byham, William & Wilson, Jeanne. **Empowered Teams.** Points of Light Foundation, Volunteer Readership. Washington, DC.

Yarbrough, Elaine. **Constructive Conflict.** Heritage Arts Publishing, 1807 Prairie Ave., Downers Grove, IL. 60515. orders: 1-800-272-8306.